CHANGING FOREVER

March 12, 1996

To Dr. Milton Mulder,

With sincere appreciation for your personal and professional interest

Sincerely

Carl Frost

CHANGING FOREVER

The Well-Kept Secret
of America's Leading
Companies

Carl F. Frost

Michigan State University Press
East Lansing

All Michigan State University Press books are produced on paper which meets the requirements of American National Standard of Information Sciences—Permanence of paper for printed materials ANSI Z39.48-1984.

Michigan State University Press
East Lansing, Michigan 48823-5202

03 02 01 00 99 98 97 96 1 2 3 4 5 6 7 8 9

Library of Congress Cataloging-in-Publication Data

Frost, Carl F.
Changing forever: the well-kept secret of America's leading companies / Carl F. Frost.
    p.   cm.
  Includes bibliographical references and index.
  ISBN 0-87013-404-3 (alk. paper)
    1. Industrial management—United States. 2. Management—Employee participa-
  tion—United States. 3. Organizational change—United States. 4. Scanlon, Joseph
  Norbert—Views on management. 5. Succcess in business—United States—Case
  Studies. I. Title.
HD70.U5F76   1995
658—dc20
                                                                    95-37632
                                                                    CIP

The Scanlon Plan Associates, a nonprofit association of organizations committed to the Frost/Scanlon principles, is proud to support the publication of this important work. We encourage readers interested in learning more about the Frost/Scanlon principles to contact us at Scanlon Plan Associates, P.O. Box 23171, Lansing, Michigan, 48909. Phone: (517) 332-8927. Email: Scanlon1@aol.com.

For

Evelyn,
wife and mother

Susan and Joe, Richard and Susie, Robert and Jane, Jackie and Bob,
our seriously dedicated children and their spouses

Carl Francis, Katie, Eric, Christopher, Megan, Peter, Danae,
our promising grandchildren

CONTENTS

FOREWORD

Odd as it may seem, I would like to begin this foreword with a quotation from Pope J. Paul II. It comes from his marvelous encyclical of 1991, "The Hundredth Year."

> The church acknowledges the legitimate role of profit as an indication that a business is functioning well. When a firm makes a profit, this means that productive factors have been properly employed and corresponding human needs have been duly satisfied. . . . in fact, the purpose of a business firm is not simply to make a profit, but is to be found in its very existence as a community of persons who in various ways are endeavoring to satisfy their basic needs and who form a particular group at the service of the whole of society. Profit is a regulator of the life of a business, but it is not the only one; other human and moral factors must also be considered, which in the long term are at least equally important for the life of a business.

Carl Frost, as a consultant, has been a teaching leader at Herman Miller, Inc., since 1949. Over those years, he was also mentor and friend to many of us who spent our careers at Herman Miller. *Changing Forever* is rooted in his professional research and practice of more than fifty years in a variety of companies and nonprofit organizations. Fifty years seems a reasonable time from which to assess results. Frost has left a legacy of results in this book, derived from responsible research and validated with extensive practice. The results of his teaching have succeeded against tough criteria over long periods, in many companies and nonprofit settings. *Changing Forever* is a bracing dose of reality.

In a number of ways, this book serves any organization's needs. It asks the right questions, describes an idea, focuses on potential, and teaches us about the role of relationships.

It is a popular, discouraging, and self-defeating practice nowadays to ask the wrong questions. We ask what is wrong with our government, our educational system, and business. This book asks, and then answers, the right question about the capitalist system. How can the *potential* of groups, individuals, and society be best realized in the capitalist system?

Frost writes about the research, practice, and evaluation of the results of participative management in a meaningful way, describing an enlightened way of working together in a market-driven system, and responding to broad areas of need. Participative management theory and practice, as taught by Frost, is the wonderful expression of the truth which states that in modern society the most effective organizations are composed of citizens, not subjects. The aim of organized work is not just to achieve our goals, but especially to reach our potential.

Expressed in subtle yet important ways in *Changing Forever* is the crucial concept that justice in organized life lies primarily in our relationships—relationships having to do with compensation (the distribution of results), opportunity, communication, identity, and access.

For those of us who will make the commitment and bring this passion to Frost's teachings, there is a wonderful beneficial surprise. Unique results, competitive advantage, and a civil culture are among the benefits. Learning to measure what matters, building community, and searching for the common good are all part of the outcome. What matters in terms of relationships within the organization also matters in our families and communities. Who counts and what counts in our organizations are the same for society at large.

But I have to say this: Frost's method is not an easy way to lead and manage. Participative management is a unique opportunity and challenge, which is difficult to practice. While the results are important and beyond debate, if executives and organizations do not comprehend, or make a commitment to these principles and processes, participative management will not work. It demands, especially of leaders, a personal competence, discipline, and passion. It is tough, but it is worth it. If you believe, as John Paul II does, that profit is not the only regulator of the life of a business, *Changing Forever* will enrich your life and the life of your organization.

Max DePree

PREFACE

This book is a momentary update in my continuing study of personal, professional, and organizational development.

Hugh DePree, former president of Herman Miller, Inc., was once asked by a prospective client, "What has Frost done for Herman Miller?" After a prolonged pause, Hugh answered, "I really can't think of anything that Frost has done for Herman Miller." The caller then asked whether I was still employed as a consultant to Herman Miller. Hugh's second answer came more quickly, "Oh, of course. You know he keeps asking the damnedest questions!"

This book is not the answer book. It is my personal and professional evaluations and distillations of candid thoughts about those "damned" questions I've been asking over the years.

The range of organizations that I have worked with gives me the confidence to suggest that perhaps the lessons I've learned are generally applicable to personal, professional, and organizational development. The awards these companies have won, their continued placement among *Fortune*'s list of the most admired companies and among the *One Hundred Best Companies to Work For in America* also give me faith that something about Scanlon and participation is worth knowing and practicing.

ACKNOWLEDGMENTS

Clark Malcolm
   Organizational treasure, gifted editor, and friend

Scanlon Plan Associates
   Lifetime opportunities from these receptive and challenging colleagues

Rick Merpi
   Video communication artist and producer of "The Scanlon Plan: A Better Way"

A business is rightly judged by its products and services—but it must also face scrutiny and judgment as to its humanity.

—D. J. DePree

INTRODUCTION

We are all aware of the proliferation of management concepts such as quality circles, Deming's program of monitoring quality processing, social technical teams, autonomous work groups, and procedures for earning the prestigious Baldrige Award. Do these programs insure the competitive survival and continued success of organizations? Joshua Hammond, president of the non-profit American Quality Foundation, sees executives mistaking the Baldrige Award procedure for a panacea and warns "it does not address key elements of business success—innovation, financial performance, and long-term planning" (*Fortune*, 1 July 1991). David Nadler, head of the Delta Consulting Group in New York and a Baldrige fan, says, "With the growing visibility of the Baldrige, there's growing misunderstanding. The goal of winning may displace the goal of achieving real quality"(*Fortune*, 1 July 1991). Of course pursuing the Baldrige Award is only one example of the ways in which American organizations are reaching out to find ways of improving their performance. In these highly competitive times, it is appropriate and challenging to ask whether the Scanlon Plan is relevant or useful today. Can it help organizations insure their survival and success any more than the profusion of other management theories?

In the 1940s and until Joe Scanlon's death in 1956, the idea that labor and management might cooperate was not commonly understood, accepted, or practiced. The advantages of labor and management cooperation were recognized by Douglas McGregor, because they seemed to embody the putative consequences of Theory Y, as contrasted with Theory X. In his pioneering book, *The Human Side of Enterprise* (1960), an early evolution of organizational development, McGregor suggests that employees' involvement and initiatives might prove more advantageous than the widely practiced "engineering" of the human factor into the workplace equation.

It was fortunate that Douglas McGregor was able to persuade Joe Scanlon to leave his position as research associate with Philip Murray, president of the United Steel Workers of America in Pittsburgh, and join the eclectic faculty at Massachusetts Institute of Technology and the Trade Unions Fellows Program at Harvard University. As John Hoerr observed in his book *And the Wolf Finally Came*, "Steel management killed the possibility of worker participation in the 1940s, and the United Steelworkers—as if embarrassed for having broached it—drove the idea into deep obscurity." But Joe Scanlon and his concept of cooperative management found an immediate and challenging milieu among such scholars as Kurt Lewin, Douglas Brown, Paul Samuelson, Charles Myers, Alex Bavelas, Irving Knickerbocker, and Mason Haire. It was exhilarating for an institution so conspicuously committed to the well-known concepts of industrial engineering to explore such a radical concept of social science and industrial relations. Kurt Lewin's work on the measurement of relational forces both adversarial and cooperative by the use of vectors whose lengths represented their respective strengths provided many models for discussion. Economists were quick to predict the impact of cooperation on productivity and profitability, though they were often frustrated by underestimating the contributions and potential of employees, once given the opportunity to participate. Russell Davenport adequately captures the spirit of this cooperative concept and its experimental applications in such organizations as LaPointe Machine Tool Company, Towle Silver Company, and Market Forge Company ("Enterprise for Everyman," *Fortune*, 1951).

Fifty years have passed since Joe Scanlon demonstrated the possibilities and potential of management and labor cooperation. Even though radical economic and social changes have occurred throughout these fifty years, it is useful to review the circumstances that surrounded the early attempts at labor-management cooperation.

Scanlon programs like those at LaPointe Machine Tool Company were generally explored as a way to address entrenched adversarial relationships and to increase productivity. Genuine threats to the survival of organizations and jobs got the attention of employees and their unions. Such threats were not publicized or explained to employees. Often, management's appeal for help came too late. Little company history or few reserves of trust existed from which to evaluate and discuss these highly emotional concerns and build a structure of cooperative relationships. Any pressure to increase productivity was seen as unilaterally benefiting management. Management and union representatives often resorted to name calling and emotional accusations in early exploratory visits. Management and union officers were challenged to recognize their contractual relationship and to decide if they had enough common interests to justify a mutual exploration of the concept of cooperation. It was essential for the union officers to keep their members informed of such an exploration, to avoid the inference of collusion or sellout. The exploratory stage climaxed with a union hall meeting of the membership to approve their union officers' pursuit of the concept of cooperation. Their approval usually came only after the organizational adversarial history had been reviewed, often cathartically, and the skepticism and suspicion of a hidden agenda had been aired.

The explorations required significant scheduled time and effort devoted to voicing honestly the perceived irrationalities of management's actions and decisions, as well as the perceived irrationalities of restrictive labor practices and negotiations. The starting point was often an armed truce, with specified limitations on topics, applications, and time.

These meetings of the cooperative program focused on manufacturing operations and the need for gains in productivity. The need to educate all employees was not considered. Employees were informed only about the volume of orders and production schedules; they were seldom informed about expected returns on the company investments in facilities or machinery. Profit as a cost of doing business was discounted. The relevance of research, development, engineering, and market possibilities was not considered part of an employee's interest or responsibility. For example, only after several years of earning bonuses on increased productivity did the LaPointe Machine Tool Company employees have the opportunity to become involved and realize the economic payoffs of more efficient equipment, as well as the personal satisfaction of working on modern, efficient, and easily maintained machines. Recognizing the need to replace their own obsolete equipment, the Screening Committee volunteered to evaluate the machinery to be auctioned at a nearby defunct machine company. Mr. Prindeville, their company president, agreed to meet with them and receive their evaluations at lunch on Saturday at noon. The employees' criteria of better quality products, higher productivity, less downtime, and less maintenance met all of Mr. Prindeville's financial criteria. These employees acted as true capital investors when given the rare opportunity and assumed responsibility for realizing the full return on the investment for the owner, as well as increased bonuses for themselves.

Another characteristic of early Scanlon plans was the emphasis on production personnel. Employees, with their unions, believed that the management staff, clerical staff, and engineers did not and could not contribute significantly to increasing productivity. Because of these beliefs and adversarial relationships, the exploration of cooperation did not include these organizational members. Unfortunately, this discrimination only reinforced the separation. Parker Pen Company, which has had long experience with a Scanlon program, has tolerated this separation of the two groups. When various overtures to integrate all employees were rejected, management matched the production productivity bonus for all supervisors, engineers, and staff members. The separate relationship seemed to be reinforced by the fact that the engineering and administrative offices were located in downtown Janesville, far away from the plant.

Other organizations adopted a two-tiered system of programs and bonus payments for productivity gains. An early version of the Motorola Participation Program (P.M.P.) separated manufacturing employees from engineering, development, fiscal, and administrative personnel. The rationale was that since managers and executives had primary responsibility for corporate profitability, and since this responsibility was far removed from the comprehension and influence of production employees, only a two-tiered program was equitable. Furthermore, as corporate profitability might at times be out of time sequence with employee performances, misunderstandings, confusion, and even resentment among production employees might arise. At the time, Motorola, as well as most other companies developing and introducing new products to the market, enjoyed the luxury of months, and even years, during which to develop and introduce new products. Immediate turnarounds in the development and delivery of new or revised products, as demanded today, were unknown. Long development times helped mask for years the need to integrate the work of all parts of the company into a single set of performance criteria.

In early Scanlon applications, representatives were elected primarily among manufacturing employees. Departmental Production Committee and Screening Committee meetings were attended principally by production or operations personnel. The agenda focused specifically on production goals and suggestions to improve quality, reduce costs, and substantiate bonus calculations. Marketing and sales people seldom entered the discussions except as a way to ensure a solid backlog of work.

The results of this preoccupation with production often became dramatically apparent. For example, at the LaPointe Machine Tool Company, the much-improved production operation ran out of backlog in the first year of the trial program. New orders required at least three or four months of engineering time before the production orders could be released into the shop. It soon became obvious that the engineers, purchasing agents, and many others directly impacted productivity. When this condition was reported at the next monthly Screening Committee meeting, Fred Lesieur, the local union president, asked for permission to meet with the engineers immediately to try to persuade them to postpone their vacations, scheduled for the next week. He was persuasive and brought back an affirmative answer to the committee within twenty minutes. Production had real priority.

Even Herman Miller, Inc., a long-time Scanlon program advocate, was initially adamant in excluding marketing and sales force members from its Scanlon program, but not because the salespeople were uninterested. In fact, the sales force asked to receive the Screening Committee Meeting minutes, to be informed, and to have some relationship with Scanlon employees. Certain executives and many production employees believed the salespeople were more than adequately remunerated and merited no additional bonus. After all, the salespeople were commissioned, sophisticated urbanites in distant commercial centers, in contrast with the working and *producing* citizens of Zeeland and Holland, Michigan.

These examples illustrate some of the characteristics of early Scanlon programs. They suggest that some of the deficiencies, such as organizational illiteracy and the lack of opportunity to accept full ownership responsibility, proved to be real obstacles to achieving changing corporate competitive objectives. The early period, through 1960, is documented in *The Scanlon Plan: A Frontier in Labor-Management Cooperation*, edited by Frederick G. Lesieur.

During this time, although Douglas McGregor left MIT to assume the presidency of Antioch College and Joe Scanlon died in 1956, the Scanlon Plan continued as the "Dream of a Steelworker." There has been no generic advocacy organization of Scanlon Plan partisans. MIT has sponsored an annual conference, usually led by Mr. Fred Lesieur, the former

United Steelworkers Local president of LaPointe Machine Tool Company and later an independent consultant. Other efforts, such as those of Tim Ross and Robert Doyle, have developed a financially oriented "gainsharing" approach. Under Jack Grayson, the American Productivity Center was established in Houston, Texas, emphasizing productivity gains. A formally constituted group of practicing companies identified themselves as the Midwest Scanlon Plan Associates in 1964, and later as Scanlon Plan Associates. Their specific commitments are to research, develop, and advocate the principles and processes consistent with the concept of cooperative relationships. Their members have been indispensable partners in the continuing development and experimental refining of the current four basic principles and their processes. Their personal and professional advocacies and the implementation of these findings have accompanied vigorous growth and conspicuous leadership in product development and services. These companies continue to earn national recognition for the innovative management of their respective marketplaces, financial investors, and, perhaps most conspicuously, the management of their human resources. Some of the most active and innovative members of the Scanlon Plan Associates are Herman Miller, Inc., the Donnelly Corporation, Motorola, Inc., Firestone Tire Company (now Bridgestone Tire Company), Boston's Beth Israel Hospital, and the Xaloy Company.

The question remains: What is the current relevance of Joe Scanlon and his dreams? It may be like asking whether Columbus should get credit for discovering America. Whether he gets or deserves the credit is not important. What is important is to identify what America is today, and then what basic principles and processes have been and are now important, if not critical, in its survival and its success. I believe organizational cooperative developments since Joe Scanlon are valid and reliable for optimistically planning tomorrow's America. I also believe that the ideas of cooperation, literacy, and equity among labor and management are as relevant and as necessary today as they ever were.

CHAPTER ONE

THE FROST-SCANLON PLAN: WHAT IT WAS, WHAT IT ISN'T, WHAT IT HAS BECOME

Joe Scanlon never thought his concept would remain unchanged. He sincerely hoped the concept of cooperation would be a promising and practical tool in organizational management, especially for its human resources in addressing a changing world. Though the concepts presented in this book have evolved out of Joe Scanlon's original idea of cooperation, they are being continuously challenged and modified. The economic, social, and political pressures, domestically and internationally, do not tolerate the luxury of organizational renewal or the maintenance of existing approaches in the management of customers, investors, or employees. On the contrary, the accelerating changes of recent decades have provided opportunities and believable imperatives to improve, innovate, and even originate organizational concepts and processes. The competent and innovative management of change is our primary hope—and hope is not joy, but the opportunity and responsibility to make the difference necessary for survival and success.

Throughout Frost-Scanlon's four functions of education, ownership, accountability, and commitment, there is a singleness of purpose applicable to every employee. The purpose is to enable all employees to *become* literate about their companies' realities, to *become* responsible in owning the problems and their solutions, to *become* personally and professionally accountable for action, and to *become* increasingly committed to personal and organizational competitive competence. Frost-Scanlon is a method for establishing such a humane process in today's organizations.

It may help to posit a checklist of what the Frost-Scanlon process is not. This list does not minimize the contributions of Douglas McGregor,

Joe Scanlon, and others. It does indicate that I believe Scanlon ideas must grow and evolve as changing realities impact organizations and their employees. I trust that the list will provide a frame of reference for presenting and evaluating the concepts of current Frost-Scanlon thinking that are meeting with some success in organizations like Herman Miller, Donnelly Corporation, Motorola, and Boston Beth Israel Hospital.

What Today's Frost-Scanlon Process Is Not

It is not a plan.
It is not an incentive system.
It is not a productivity gain-sharing scheme.
It is not a manufacturing or operations tactic.
It is not a management program.
It is not a human-resources program or responsibility.
It is not the chief executive officer's or president's project.
It is not the creation of a consultant.
It is not static.
It is not self-managed.
It is not packaged.
It is not contractual or contracted.
It is not easy.
It is not optional.
It has no guarantees.
It is not impersonal.
It does not grant or allow personal privilege.
It is not adversarial.
It is not a system of renewal.
It is not a luxury.
It is not an add-on activity.
It is not for every employee.
It is not for every professional.
It is not for every company or organization.

What is today's Frost-Scanlon process? This developmental process enables management to create a rational working environment in which each employee's dignity is recognized and every employee's potential is challenged in achieving the organization's objectives.

Today's Frost-Scanlon Plan Process

It is a personal development process.
It is a professional development process.
It is an organizational development process.
The process begins as a companywide exploration.
It is uniquely developed, accepted, and implemented in each company.
It is ongoing.
It involves all employees.
It is integral to all of the organization's functions.
It is authenticated by external imperatives.
It is dynamic and responsive to changing imperatives.
It is a way to survive.

The primary point to emphasize is the difference, at least as I have experienced it, between a plan and a process. The dictionary definition of a plan is a "detailed scheme, method, or program worked out beforehand for the accomplishment of an objective." In contrast, the dictionary definition of a process is "a series of actions, ongoing movement, changes, or functions that bring about an end or result." The definition of a plan identifies a preconceived and packaged program for organizational development superimposed by authority or external experts. The definition of a process identifies an evolutionary procedure developed by recognizing situational needs and then applying and testing possible solutions to meet changing demands. The process definition suggests continuous active member involvement in authoring, creating, and innovating answers or solutions.

The Scanlon Plan Associates Logo (see fig. 1), designed by Rob Hugel, captures the essence of these differences between the static quality of a plan and the dynamics of a process.

Teamwork
Give and Take
Back and Forth
Two-Way Communication
Connectedness
Forward Together
Purposeful—Directed
Dynamic—Never Ending
Three-Dimensional Organization
No Rigid Hierarchical Structure
Synergy

Figure 1. Scanlon Plan Associates Logo

The next step is to differentiate the Frost-Scanlon process from any other organizational development program, recognizing that many other programs are available and are successful. The Frost-Scanlon process is a useful tool for creating healthy, competitively productive organizations. The process is based on four assumptions:

Change is inevitable, and change is our only hope.
Education is the best investment in achieving change.
Current behavior is a consequence of previous treatment.
Every person and organization is in the state of becoming.

The process is based on four sequential principles:

Identity
Participation
Equity
Competence

The process is implemented through four successive procedures:

Education
Ownership
Accountability
Commitment

The Frost-Scanlon process differs markedly from other organizational schemes in the definition of these four basic behavioral principles and the resolute development and implementation of the functions that fulfill these principles. Another critical difference in the Frost-Scanlon process is the essential sequence of these evolutionary actions that assures the achievement of results.

The four principles and their processes will be presented in this book in this sequence and will demonstrate the unique but expected cumulative effect of the Frost-Scanlon process.

Personal, Professional, and Organizational Development

Principle	**Process**
Identity:	*Education*:
Doing the right job	Literacy: Industry competition
Doing the job right	Literacy: Organization's mandate
Participation:	*Ownership*:
Opportunity given by management	Initiative
Responsibility taken by employees	Involvement
Equity:	*Accountability*:
Customers/clients/patients	Personal
Stockholders/owners	Professional
Employees	Organizational
Competence:	*Commitment*:
Personal	Personal
Professional	Professional
Organizational	Organizational

11

CHAPTER TWO

THE FIRST PRINCIPLE: IDENTITY

Competitive Reality Literacy

The first principle is identity: the knowledge, understanding, and acceptance of the fact that reality places survival at risk—personally, professionally, and organizationally. Survival of the fittest, the watchword of biological evolution, has genuine and pressing relevance to organizations as well as to biological species. Competitive realities dictate the conditions for survival. Polonius's advice, "Know thyself and to thyself be true," is the essence of personal reality and personal identity. Identity is developed from and focused on reality—the fundamental truth from birth to death for individuals as well as organizations and institutions.

Birth and survival depend on recognizing and coping with essential life-signs of reality. For example, one of our greatest tragedies in America is the excessively high mortality rate of infants. We in the United States rank twenty-sixth among developed nations. The primary cause of this is the failure to know and respond to the critical conditions for successful birthing. Given the ignorance and unreal perceptions of many young mothers, the consequences are predictable.

The primary cause of organizational failure and death is management's failure to educate employees about reality and the employees' inability to understand and respond to the competitive demands for survival. Given the ignorance of competitive realities among many organizational members and their unreal perceptions of personal threats to the organization, the consequences are predictable.

13

When I think of identity and the types of things that identity provides in a Scanlon company, I think of the information that people need to do their jobs, from a corporate point of view, an understanding of the strategies, an identity with corporate culture, understanding how the company operates and works and functions. I think identity also comes with being able to understand where one fits into an organization as well as the work that organization does, how one fits into the total and the contributions that individuals and the organization make, whatever level that person is at. That's what identity means to me.*

—*Wayne, corp. business systems, Herman Miller, Inc.*

At the Wolverine World Wide Corporation, exploration of the principle of identity quickly revealed the employees' disparate perceptions of their company's changing reality.

President Adolph Krause had somewhat facetiously selected a giant, orange basset hound as the new company logo. This friendly, oversized hound dog image soon captured the affections of customers, symbolizing to them the comfort of Hush Puppies, Wolverine World Wide's new product and the first shoe to be manufactured entirely from pig skins. The new product was soon a success.

The thirteen shoe manufacturing units saw their changed personal and professional reality to be a frustrating inability to keep up with the enthusiastic and accelerating demand for Hush Puppies. They also saw that they depended on a single tannery, which had patented the process of transforming one-piece pig hides into quality shoes and gloves.

The Rockford Tannery employees saw little reason to change. Their reality consisted of a pride in their group, a genuine esprit de corps, despite the malodorous working conditions. After all, they were the only tannery in the United States equipped to process pig hides in single pieces. They frequently referred to their business as "making a lady's purse out of a sow's ear." The success of Hush Puppies simply meant more work for them. Yet the quality of their work was increasingly unacceptable to the Wolverine Shoe manufacturing divisions and to customers wanting more perfectly matched leathers on the uppers of their new Hush

---

*This quotation and others like it scattered through the text are taken from interviews conducted by Rick Merpi in preparation for the videotape, "The Scanlon Plan: A Better Way," produced in 1987.

Puppies. Somehow, these two perceptions of current competitive reality had to be brought into sync.

Employee representatives from the tannery convened their monthly meeting in a nearby shopping mall. At the beginning of the next session, the general manager of the tannery gave money to each representative with the instruction to buy the best pair of casual shoes in the mall. When the representatives regrouped, not one had bought a pair of Hush Puppies! They discovered that their own product was inferior in the market. The tannery employees had learned dramatically how illiterate they had been about their competitive reality. They then accepted the opportunity and, more important, the responsibility to change. With more sophisticated technology and daily collaboration with the manufacturing units, the tannery employees began to share in the reality facing Wolverine World Wide. Within two months, inspections of hides were cut from two to one, the quality and availability of hides for Hush Puppies increased, and the manufacturing and tannery employees began to share a real corporate identity.

The demand for entrepreneurs, executives, and employees to anticipate, understand, and respond to their own competitive realities is pressing in the birth, survival, and maturation of industrial ventures. Current bankruptcy rates document the consequences of organizational illiteracy and its resulting incompetence. Personal, professional, and organizational literacies (the four principles of the Frost-Scanlon process apply equally in three dimensions: personal, professional, and organizational) compel us to define and establish identity and to comprehend competitive realities.

I feel like they know that something has to change. . . . I'm not going to let them be that blind, because it's on television every day. So-and-so closed down. This company closed down. When things like this start happening, people's eyes have to come open. When another tire plant closes down, the bottom line to the employees should be, "Why did it close down?"

—Wallace, warehouse employee, Firestone Tire

We often speak of and resent the harsh realities of life, and we must come to grips with these ineluctable conditions. They belong to each individual and organization. They cannot be transferred. Notice, I did not say they cannot be *shared*. In spite of all the negative feelings and resentment of competitive realities, I believe it is wholesome and essential to recognize candidly that reality is all we have to share. To share that reality appropriately is a genuine favor. Facing up to reality should be viewed as a genuine opportunity and accepted as a challenging responsibility. We must, however, honestly acknowledge that resentment of and resistance to changing realities and their demands are common reactions. True leaders are seldom remembered for asking their followers to remain the way they are. We revere Abraham Lincoln not for perpetuating slavery but for ending it.

Douglas McGregor often asked this about reality: "What are you going to do about it *now*?" He dramatically demonstrated this attitude for me at a formal dinner he hosted with Joe Scanlon in the staid decorum of the Harvard Club "across the river." The guests were the management executives and the union officers (five members of each group) of the Baldwin Locomotive Company from Baltimore. They had spent a long day visiting the Lapointe Machine Tool Company operations in Hudson, Massachusetts. During dinner, the two groups became embroiled in an emotional shouting match. Douglas McGregor quietly left the dinner table and retreated to a convenient divan to resume cheese and crackers with another dry martini. Suddenly the guests realized their host had absented himself from their table. In some embarrassment, they urged him to return to the table. He nonchalantly complied. After an uncomfortable silence, McGregor quietly asked, "What are you going to do *now*?" The question brought a dramatic calm of rationality. The opportunity for needed change had been provided. *Now*, would they accept the responsibility?

In the principle of identity, reality is the essential element. To be ignorant or deprived of reality is to be organizationally illiterate. Illiterate behavior, the consequence of illiteracy, has predictable personal, professional, and organizational impacts. In organizations where employees do not know their customers and their competitive demands, can we legitimately expect them to become superior in performance and service? The answer is no. Yet, how often do organizations fault the behavior of employees without addressing the root cause—or without giving individuals the knowledge to change, to say nothing of the imperatives to change?

. . . but you've got to have the opportunity to be literate. You have to have the opportunity to identify with it. You've got to have an opportunity and system, I believe, to participate.

—*Michele, People Department, Herman Miller, Inc.*

Everyone deserves *the chance* to become responsible. Given the opportunity for literacy, the individual must make a choice—to become responsible or not. The choice made here depends on personal skill or attitude, which should be recognized as critical in the interpretation of employees' behaviors. You will also notice that I use the words "to become," because they document a change in the employees' behaviors once they have the opportunity to know, understand, and comprehend the competitive facts of their own organizational reality.

Responsibility and Accountability

The most apparent consequence of illiteracy is the inability or unwillingness—the failure—to become responsible. As you might expect, once a person is not responsible, the inability or unwillingness to be or to become accountable follows, as the night does the day. If the opportunity is genuinely and convincingly provided and responsibility sincerely and competently accepted, however, then we can confidently expect that accountability for one's job will be recognized and welcomed. In fact, only an overt acknowledgment of accountability can authenticate a person's acceptance of responsibility. Responsibility without meaningful accountability is not only an abortion of the processes, but also a personal and professional insult to employees.

Commitment

After the failure to become responsible and accountable, reality illiteracy results in a failure or refusal to commit to change. Commitment, on the contrary, should be the third consequence of literacy. After a person accepts the opportunity to become responsible, he or she must make a personal and professional commitment to improve performance, practices, or relationships—in short, to change for the better. Meaningful commitment is seldom spontaneous. In response to a genuine opportunity

17

for *me* to *own* the problem, it must be derived from the conviction that *I* and *my organization* must change.

I think everyone has a responsibility to initiate change. Everybody! If you believe in the company and if you believe you have something to offer, then by golly, you better be involved in influencing change.
                    —*Bob, manufacturing engineering, Herman Miller, Inc.*

Identity relates every employee personally and professionally to his or her own reality as authenticated and experienced in the organization. Individualized and personalized reality is the only valid and reliable rationale for an employee to work at surviving and succeeding. Only after understanding reality could the tannery employees serving the fabricating divisions begin to change. Education insures that everyone shares the same organizational and competitive realities.

Do not conclude too quickly that the simplicity of the identity concept makes it too obvious to be acceptable or useful. A strong sense of personal, professional, and organizational identity is mandatory and primary. Reality's identity accepts and purposefully accounts for a full range of individual differences in behavior and motivation. Consider for a moment why an employee inadvertently ships the wrong product to a customer; why a salesperson discounts a product below cost; why an executive accepts kickbacks or remuneration hundreds of times more than the average income of employees. Are these behaviors attributable to confusion or ignorance of basic facts about reality? There is no confusion; only ignorance of the consequences lies at the root of these behaviors. The employee is ignorant of a customer's demand for quality products and on-time delivery (or of the effect of his mistake on the company); the executive is ignorant of the effect of his compensation on equity in the corporation. Perhaps, as John Gardner recently observed, we "have become so mesmerized by our (personal) or group interests that we have forgotten how to act in common."

As far as identity goes . . . we spend a lot of time letting our people know as much about this company as we possibly can. As a result, our employees know what direction the company is headed in, and that includes opening up the books, what management has decided and why.

—Michele, People Department, Herman Miller, Inc.

Why? I suggest that ignorance of common, organizational realities is the cause. Alternative explanations leave us no hope for survival. There is a genuine need to determine, define, and articulate these realities so that an employee can take the time to do it right the first time, so that a salesperson can keep the required level of profitability in sight at all times, and so that an executive can avoid disheartening the entire organization with inequitable behavior. Above all, if we are to change, we must all understand the constraints as well as the outcomes.

I think if anything we were probably given more information when things were bad. We had to be made aware of what the company was facing. We were privy to discussions on where the company was going to go during this undetermined length of automotive business downturn. We were given the responsibility as employees to respond to these needs of the company.

—Jim, manufacturing and engineering group, Donnelly Corp.

When I refer to organizational reality, I'm speaking of the clarity and believability of truth. Truth really is in the eye of the beholder, and we must begin with what an individual is, what he knows and understands, so that his truth matches the realities of the external world. Education has been the traditional process through which we learn to know the truth or, in this case, the competitive realities that compel change.

Education and Change

When we speak of literacy, we in America recognize education as the process that serves us well to produce it, at least historically. We have prided ourselves on universal education, recognizing that a democratic system will not function with an illiterate populace. And yet, our citizens are illiterate regarding the costs of infant mortality, drug-impacted births, and terminally ill senior citizens, which are significantly greater problems here than in other industrialized nations. Historically, education has been our most promising national investment. However, as we become a more globally conspicuous nation, what does the worldwide experience and database tell us? Are we globally literate regarding both social and economic factors? Are we able to teach and to learn so as to become literate, responsible, accountable, and committed to managing our continually changing realities?

John Kenneth Galbraith said recently at the International Labor Organization meeting in Geneva that "an educated populace is the first requirement of economic progress." He went on to say, "there is no literate population that is poor, no illiterate population that is other than poor." The Japanese seem particularly literate in the economic, social, and political competitive realities, not only in Japan, but around the world. Such a literate workforce and culture have proved to be a tangible asset for the Japanese carmakers.

Literacy—I think it gives us a real edge. I think that one of John Donnelly's favorite things to say was that if you explain it to people, they will be fine. I don't think that is necessarily true, but I do think that if you increase the literacy, keep the reality in front of people all the time, and you really are participative in terms of listening to what people have to say, ideas that are acted on, all of that, I think it gives you an enormous advantage over people who operate in a closed environment.
—Kay, systems development, Donnelly Corp.

Realities suggest—no, demand—that we change! The current wake-up calls or warnings of the futurists document that change is common and everywhere. Life from birth to death is a continuing journey where we experience and cope with change just to survive, even more so to succeed. Is the failure to change simply another example of unfaithfulness to oneself and infidelity to the truth? Reality is a changing and often threatening challenge. By denying it, as when we fail to accept that we have gotten older, we sometimes lose too soon the capacity to cope—and that, too, is a genuine, though regrettable, change. The story of the United States is replete with examples of industrial, commercial, social, religious, and healthcare organizations that all too slowly and sometimes never recognized that irrefutable reality demands change.

A reluctance to face up to reality and institute change is not limited to industrial organizations. Consider the blatant personal and professional disarray of the financial markets, banks, and insurance companies. Their supposedly innovative adventures did not account for real and radical changes in the economy, land values, and financial markets. Junk bonds, bank failures, the savings and loan scandals, and simple executive greed—the consequences of an inability or unwillingness to recognize and to respond to the reality demands of doing the right job and doing the job right—are now national tragedies.

We are facing a new kind of competitive reality. It is a time of major change in the marketplace, but it is also a huge time of a lot of change internally. . . . That is a major leap. If the next five-year plan holds we will double again in five years. We are not used to growing at that rate, and it is a real adjustment.
—Kay, systems development, Donnelly Corp.

Another national concern is the health care industry. As citizens and members of organizations, we cannot afford the escalating costs of health care. Who is now defining the right job for the institutions in research, teaching, and health care delivery? It is not an isolated industry concern. We must all—users, providers, and service institutions—become genuinely literate so that we may become responsible and accountable. Together we must define and do the right job for the health system. I'm hopeful that national leaders will concentrate on this task.

With changing events and perspectives, there has been a trend or inclination to review where we have been, a yearning to discover who we were and thereby find our roots. In this pursuit we welcomed John Gardner's book, *Self-Renewal: The Individual and the Innovative Society.* Many qualities support the idea that self-renewal might be the process to give perspective, direction, and momentum to organizational development. Gardner's book and his intriguing message are special personal and professional contributions that I recommend enthusiastically. In fact, in 1964, as I departed for a two-year university opportunity at the University of Nigeria In Nsukka, I sent eighteen copies to special executives. It was worthwhile studying then, and *Self-Renewal* is still on my recommended list.

21

With special and utmost respect for John Gardner, however, I question his thesis at this time. I am challenged by Gardner's foreword:

> Heraclitus observed that "No one steps twice into the same river"; and twenty-five centuries later thinkers are still rediscovering the inescapable reality of change. Life and the world keep flowing and evolving.

Life and the world keep flowing and changing as we individually and collectively "step into" them. In view of this idea and, more particularly, the overwhelming personal and organizational evidence that change is both impelling and compelling, we must not be seduced into thinking we can renew, go back, retread, or reinvent. Renewal is a luxury we cannot afford. Real change is our only hope.

If these observations have some merit, what message will allow us, our organizations, and our society to become genuinely literate, responsible, accountable, and committed? The message is simply that change is as real as birth and death; change is the only context in which to manage our personal, professional, and organizational worlds.

Doing the Right Job: Effectiveness

Not ignoring the personal and professional implications of the identity concept, let us focus on the organization. The initial reality question is *identifying* the right job for the organization (Doing the right job is Peter Drucker's definition of effectiveness.). We have watched the automotive industry struggle with this question belatedly and ineptly for the last two decades. They are finding that their disregarding, discounting, and denial of the reality of automobile manufacturing in the 1970s and 1980s have disenfranchised their employees in learning to deal with changed and changing realities. Only recently have they begun to involve their employees in a refreshing acknowledgment of reality and a serious commitment to change.

To avoid damning the entire automotive industry, let me insert a statement from one of its successful suppliers. Dwane Baumgardner, the chairperson and chief executive officer of the Donnelly Corporation: (*Wall Street Transcript On-Line*, 29 April 1991)

> Our global market position goes back many, many years. We've been supplying the European market for over 20 years and we've been supply-

ing the Japanese home market for over 15 years. We were well positioned to start gaining business with the transplants when they arrived in the U.S. during the late 1970s and early 1980s and we're doing business now with nearly all of the transplants today.

The opportunity is to get more content on each vehicle. Our philosophy has been to do that through adding value and the introduction of new products. . . .

Our growth in the past has been fueled by both new products and adding value to existing products. For example, many years ago, we primarily supplied only the mirror glass for the industry. The glass was coated, cut to the shape and, in the case of the prismatic mirror, we ground the glass as well. These mirrors sold for approximately $.50 to $1.00. Then we began supplying complete inside mirror assemblies.

Now, instead of supplying only the prism, we sell the entire standard mirror assembly for a little over $2.00. Adding lights to that mirror increased its value and sells for about four or five times the standard mirror. . . .

Donnelly innovated the Modular Window concept in the mid 70s. It was a great advantage for carmakers because it offered the industry lower cost systems, higher quality, and more design freedom. . . . Again, it's a new product that we innovated, gained market acceptance for, now it's in the rapid growth phase of its product life cycle.

All of these examples add up to new products and added value!

These exciting twenty years of continuous improvement and success are genuinely noteworthy. However, Donnelly's ability and commitment to survive and succeed were inaugurated in 1952, when John Fenlon Donnelly decided that the right job for the Donnelly Company was not fabricating magnificent engraved mirrors for the home and commercial facilities, but supplying the automotive industry. He quickly learned that the leaders of the automobile companies were ruthlessly demanding. General Motors required that Mr. Donnelly be available in his office between two and four o'clock on Friday afternoons to receive their decisions about what product to manufacture and the volume of production for the following week. This threatening and importunate intrusion motivated Mr. Donnelly to attempt to demonstrate his company's ability to do the job right to GM's and Donnelly's other customers' complete satisfaction.

It was not an accident that Mr. Donnelly introduced his employees to the Scanlon Plan in 1952 as a way of helping them become meaningfully

23

literate about these demanding realities. He documented the process in the *Harvard Business Review* in January 1977. In time, the Donnelly Corporation had the responsibility of supplying 100 percent of the rearview prismatic mirrors to General Motors, as well as to other automotive customers. Donnelly shipped double-trailer-loads of the mirrors every week to its Detroit customers; the customers *annually* returned to Donnelly one stationwagon-load of rejects. This record, a real achievement, was recognized and rewarded. The company has earned the highest awards from Chrysler, Ford, and General Motors. Most recently, they earned General Motors' highest awards on the Five Targets for Excellence: 1992 Leadership, Costs, Technology, Quality, and Delivery— The Mark of Excellence. The awards are only the visible signs of years of work at Donnelly to educate employees, involve them in the business, and enlist their help in meeting the compelling demands of competitive reality.

Forty years after Mr. Donnelly's recognition and acceptance of the need to change, chief executive officer Dwane Baumgardner is available not just on Friday afternoons, but twenty-four hours a day, seven days a week, to hear and respond to General Motors, as well as Ford Motor Company, Chrysler, Honda, Nissan, and Toyota. The eternal demands for change improved quality, created shorter delivery times, and reduced prices. As was widely publicized at the time, Mr. Lopez, newly appointed General Motors executive vice president, recently gave the edict that every internal and external supplier must submit, *within one week*, reduced prices on their respective parts of at least fifteen percent. There is little confusion in that mandate. It illustrates the Motorola maxim: "If you don't like surprises, you are living in the wrong century."

An appealing example of an organization with a conspicuous history of doing the right job is the Motorola Corporation. Many people will recall the company's decision to stop producing Quasar televisions. At the time, the public questioned the company's rationale. This decision was only a small part of Motorola's plan to establish and fortify itself as number one in electronic technology. This, they decided, was their right job. History reports that Motorola earned the position, lost it to a domestic competitor, and then regained it—all through changes in response to the dictates of competitive reality. Motorola recognized early that their reality was a global challenge. They learned that competitive reality welcomes successful breakthroughs for a moment and then expects another advance and breakthrough.

A visit to the Motorola Museum is a convincing documentary of that organization's ability and willingness to commit itself to total organizational literacy. The entire company aggressively continues to determine and define the right job for Motorola, committing 3 percent of its annual budget to allowing every employee to undergo a minimum of two days of schooling/training every year. Even those employees with established tenure and professional credentials are actively committed to becoming increasingly literate about their business and its realities. Education—not coercion—is still our most promising process and investment. If education results in genuine literacy, there will be no confusion over purpose or performance.

The commitment to literacy for all employees is symbolized and embodied in Motorola University, an ingenious integration of available community educational resources and Motorola's extensive educational and training resources. The program is genuinely personalized for all 104,000 production and professional employees. It is essential, if Motorola employees are to do the right job today and prepare for changed jobs in the future.

Doing the Job Right: Efficiency

The second factor of identity is doing the job right (Doing the job right is Peter Drucker's definition of efficiency.). Precise, articulate, and increasingly forthright in establishing their criteria for acceptable quality and service, customers are the primary shapers of organizational reality. Quality and service at reduced cost have become the critical benchmarks for survival; customers are increasingly resistant to handling any rejects. I might add to Mr. Drucker's definition: "doing the job right *the first time*." Several years ago, this customer imperative inspired Mr. Robert Galvin's organizational challenge "to go for perfection." As a consequence, Motorola set literacy as a goal, accepted the challenge of doing the job right, and became one of the original recipients of the prestigious Baldrige Award.

Winning the Baldrige Award was not the major accomplishment. The real achievement was educating every employee to know that past performance of two or three sigma of quality was no longer good enough. Customers were only satisfied with six-sigma quality performance, now the minimum standard for all Motorola employees. At Motorola, there is no confusion about doing the right job and the criteria for doing that job right. There is still absolute fidelity to the process of educating every employee, which qualifies them to meet the criteria required by business

25

now. As a sign of knowing the Motorola corporate identity, every employee carries a personal "calling" card (fig. 2).

OUR FUNDAMENTAL OBJECTIVE
(Everyone's Overriding Responsibility)

Total Customer Satisfaction

 **MOTOROLA**

KEY BELIEFS—*how we will always act*
• Constant Respect for People
• Uncompromising Integrity

KEY GOALS—*what we must accomplish*
• Increased Global Market Share
• Best in Class
   —*People*
   —*Marketing*
   —*Technology*
   —*Product*
   —*Manufacturing*
   —*Service*

KEY INITIATIVES—*how we will do it*
• Six Sigma Quality
• Total Cycle Time Reduction
• Product and Manufacturing Leadership
• Probe Improvement
• Participate Management Within, and
  Cooperation Between Organizations

Figure 2. Motorola, Inc. Organizational Identity

The process of identifying the right job and doing the job right has been a primary moving force in Herman Miller, Inc.'s early and continuing success. Their achievements have earned them, among other things, *Fortune* magazine's designation as one of America's Ten Most Admired Companies. As a company, Herman Miller has embraced innovation and the fulfillment of change.

I think it's important to understand the goals and the strategies so that what I'm working on is the right thing and that it directly supports the goals and strategies, because a lot can happen in an organization if those goals and strategies are not communicated. People go off in their own direction and can waste a lot of resources.

—Wayne, corporate business systems, Herman Miller, Inc.

Herman Miller founder D. J. DePree became convinced in the 1930s that traditional household furniture, highly ornate reproductions of earlier designs, of which Herman Miller was just another manufacturer, was dishonest in design and dysfunctional in use. The creators of new designs—designers like Gilbert Rohde, George Nelson, Charles Eames, and Alexander Girard—flourished at Herman Miller precisely because DePree, and then his son, Hugh, committed themselves to determining, defining, and producing (articulating) the right job for Herman Miller. Then they called upon the wonderfully skilled employees of Herman Miller to do the job right. Hugh DePree documents the management practices that led to a strong sense of identity in the company in his book *Business as Unusual.* In his words, "The difference at Herman Miller is not the lengthened shadow of one man and not the talents of an elite group of managers. The difference is the energy beamed from thousands of unique contributions by people who understand, accept, and are committed to the idea that they can make a difference." The collaborative achievements of Herman Miller and internationally recognized designers exemplify the personal, professional, and organizational results of a strong sense of identity. The quality was officially recognized by the Smithsonian Institution's major presentation, "The Age of Conscience," featuring D. J. DePree's leadership.

Another conspicuous consequence of that unique collaboration is today's office furniture industry, largely a result of Herman Miller's willingness to accept change. It was Herman Miller's Robert Propst who ingeniously recognized that industrial and commercial America was changing; for the first time in history, more men and women were employed in offices than in manufacturing plants and mills. It was and is truly a revolution. Herman Miller became the first company to educate the corporate decision makers in America not only about the need for change, but also about the most innovative ways to implement that change. Mr. Robert Propst's book, *The Office: A Facility Based on Change*, is a classic statement of the need for change and the opportunities provided by change.

Time: Past, Present, and Future

In the process of educating employees to customers' ideas of doing the right job and doing the job right, three facts need to be established to assure a literacy that can substantiate the need to change.

First, present competitive realities usually offer clear, compelling reasons to change. These reasons are all *external* imperatives, because the customer has the prerogative of accepting or rejecting the product or service. Investors are external to the company, committed to gaining the best returns on their capital investments in the company's facilities, technology, and systems. Loyalty is not an investment criterion; investors have the freedom to abandon a ship—and often do—at the slightest sign of a leak. Competent personnel are recruited from the outside marketplace. They usually have several employment opportunities. The company must prove to be an attractive employment opportunity. It must be accepted as a given that customers, investors, and employees have available and attractive alternatives to any one organization that they may take at any time.

Know our competition? Oh sure. You got your Goodyear plants, you got your Michelin, you got your B. F. Goodrich, you got your Uniroyals, and you know some of these companies are real big and there's some not so big. But every tire that somebody else sells is a tire that we don't sell—and you have all your imports coming in. All of these are our competition!

—Wallace, warehouse employee, Firestone Tire

Second, past performances, past practices, and past relationships are no longer adequate or appropriate—in fact, they are without doubt obsolete. Current personal performance must be *not only better but different*. It must change in kind, not merely in degree. Renewal will not suffice; only change will do. How I do my assignment is a professional issue, but the process must be ever more efficient and ever more technically sound and innovative. My relationships to others—customers,

28

supervisors, and fellow employees—must change; this will allow the organization to survive. If employees are not convinced that their past performances, practices, and relationships are genuinely obsolete, then there will be no reason to pursue any program for change. For employees not convinced of this fact, competitive realities are not important and change is an arbitrary imposition by management.

People saw that they were more a part of Firestone than before, instead of just being employees. They now had decisions, or had the ability to make decisions that the company would honor. . . . So, I think and I feel like that the employees felt a closer relationship and I think that management started revealing more.

—Don, machine tool operator, Firestone Tire

Management must take the time to document and diligently verify that past personal performance is no longer adequate. For example, when evidence had been shared from a key customer that past quality was no longer acceptable and that new skills and technical standards were therefore being implemented, a long-tenured employee informed her manager that inasmuch as she was four years from retirement, it would not be worthwhile for the company to train her. The manager quietly informed her that he could not assure her continued employment after that year, because she would not have the requisite skills to satisfy the customer's new quality demands. She then understood the new reality, accepted it as a personal "given," gladly participated in the training program, and genuinely welcomed her achievements and new qualifications.

It is also essential for management to recognize, admit, and confront situations in which personal and professional competencies are absent or grossly inadequate. John Donnelly, in the second year of his company's participative program, was confronted with data filtered from employees that his operations manager had become incompetent and a serious handicap. Mr. Donnelly was surprised, and he sincerely challenged the information. Donnelly emotionally defended the person by recalling that he had been the operations manager for seventeen years. He claimed, "he has been absolutely loyal through good times and difficult times. I have counted on him." After further discussion and reflection, Mr. Donnelly was asked to consider that loyalty and longevity are no substitutes for competence. Past performance, practices, and relationships were truly

29

obsolete. Happily, this gentleman became one of the local Ford sales agency's most successful salesmen and enjoyed another long career.

Third, organizations need to develop a unique position of superiority in the competitive marketplace. A unique identity is the reality of life, beginning with our personal "day one." Without a reason for being, organizations will quickly receive the following message from their customers: "You are no longer necessary!" External competition challenges all of us personally, professionally, and organizationally to become competitively competent, hopefully for all of the right reasons. Therefore, if the organization, beginning with an employee's first day of employment, does not establish a wholesome and realistic attitude toward the future, toward organizational survival, and toward success and excellence, it will not be serving its members.

Leader as Educator

If a leader is to serve an organization, and to put the company's needs before his or her own considerations, presenting a clear and convincing picture of competitive reality is paramount. Yet officers in most organizations have not looked on employee literacy as their primary responsibility. They have not taken a conspicuous role in defining for their companies "what day it is" and the right job and the competitive criteria for doing the job right. The role of the organizational educator is often delegated to subordinates or, worse, left to chance. Organizational education should become one of the leader's most challenging and productive opportunities and responsibilities. Omission or neglect of this duty denies the lifelong realities of change and the lifelong challenge, met through education, of becoming something we never were before. The purpose of teaching is not limited to telling; its purpose is to enable and facilitate learning. To understand this, simply consider the roots of two words, education and instruction. Instruction derives from two Latin words meaning "to pile up." This is not a task for leaders. Education derives from two Latin words meaning "to draw out." This is what leaders-as-educators must do: draw out the best in their followers by helping them see the problem and urging them toward problem ownership.

In building a strong sense of identity in an organization and in educating its members as to the reality they face, leaders are critical. Max DePree, in *Leadership Is an Art*, points out and illustrates key nuances in the execution of that singular role. My own experience in a Nigerian village, to which DePree refers briefly, reaffirmed for me the importance and potential of personal, professional, and organizational identity, even in such a different cultural setting. Nigeria is a nation of one hundred million people living in an area the size of Texas and divided into two hundred forty indigenous tribes, each with its own unique language. Even after hundreds of years, tribal identities are distinctly preserved through a continual process of education, though not in the same sense as we think of education in the United States. Responsibility for the educational process is ceremonially conferred upon three elders, blessed and authenticated by the powers of the tribal *juju*. A primary duty of the elders is to tell the tribe's unique story, so that all members know who they are, where they came from, their present circumstance, and what may be in their future. During my years in the village of Nsukka, electricity was limited and undependable. The evening telling of the tribal history and culture had the undivided attention of the villagers around a small fire or flickering candle.

The tribal story consisted of three episodes told in the same sequence. The story of the past included the report of great events of achievement and survival, but also of failures, famines, and tribal warfare. It is human drama at its best, narrated by authentic leaders. Even the periodic historic sale of some members into slavery was narrated, the sale described as the most humane way to avoid mass starvation during extended droughts. The details and repetition of the tribal history established its veracity and mutuality. These events helped the storytellers to establish the unique identity of the tribe.

The story of present circumstances dealt with the critical and daily need for water and wood and their limited availability. A great part of each day was spent searching for wood and traveling miles for water. (One of the best available water sources within a couple of miles was the spigot behind our home. Small boys and women gathered at daybreak for their daily supply.) A continuous caution was to save enough seed yam on the drying racks to plant next year's crop. Survival was an urgent part of this tribe's daily story. Every member had to understand the urgent circumstances and to manage time and limited resources.

The third part of the story was the hopes and plans for one or two of their village children to go to school. At that time there was only one secondary school in the Northern Region, the largest of the three geographical regions of Nigeria. Education was the most promising means to a better tribal future. The singularly advantaged child selected by the elders and subsidized by the tribe always came back to the village upon completion of his education and built a cinder-block house of personal commitment to the tribe. Even though the graduates were usually employed elsewhere, they returned in December to counsel with the elders and their village's extended families. This primitive but fundamental education program entrusted to the three elders has enabled their peoples to survive and strive toward something better. Incidentally, the term *elders* does not connote age or seniority, it represents the leadership hallmarks of trust and competence.

Storytelling in Organizations

Leaders in organizations are not unlike these tribal elders. The identity they build through perpetuating the history, identifying the present, and envisioning the future of their groups is absolutely necessary to the life of the organizations they lead. In thinking about literacy, education, organizations, and leaders, I suggest that we ask three questions:

Is there a tribal or organizational story to tell? Past? Present? And future?
Should the story be told?
Who is most qualified to tell the story?

As you reflect on the challenges of these three questions, you can identify a number of great storytellers. John Gardner was a great storyteller for the Carnegie Corporation, for the United States Department of Health, Education and Welfare, and as founder and chairperson of Common Cause (the citizen's lobby). D. J. DePree, the founder of Herman Miller, Inc., was the storyteller of the Age of Conscience, influencing the company and the office furniture industry. *Business Week* (25 October 1991) states:

Fifty times a year, at one factory or office after another, Corning Inc. Chairman James R. Houghton gives pretty much the same spiel. Quality, quality, quality. World-class. Customer focus. Worker participation. At each site, a sermon for the employee ranks, then a no-nonsense performance review with local managers.

Tiresome? Just a bit. Houghton has been preaching this gospel since 1983. But he keeps at it. "After eight years, if I stop talking about quality now, it would be a disaster," he says.

32

And again from *Business Week,*

> Chief Executive Officer I. MacAllister Booth of the Polaroid Corporation, who is shooting for a tenfold gain in customer satisfaction over the next five years and a halving of the time it takes new products to break even, "Managing for quality isn't easy. It requires active, unwavering leadership from the chief executive officer, organizational change of the largest order—and time."
>
> "Yet sometimes, resistance to change is so stubborn as to require a cultural wake-up call. Polaroid was, for decades, one of the nation's most innovative and successful companies . . . . Now, there's an implication that we've been asleep at the switch for twenty years. That's not easy for me or the rest of the folks in the company to accept."

Paul Galvin earlier, and now his son, Robert Galvin, the great storytellers of Motorola, continually challenge all employees to do the right job and to do the job right, striving even toward the point of perfection. Their personal visibility documents their vision, competence, and commitment in serving Motorola. As company educators, these gentlemen fulfill my definition of leadership: A leader is the person who is *perceived by the followers* as their *best means available* to get them *where they need to go* at this *particular time.*

We have discussed the principle of identity and the process of developing and assuring employee literacy largely in the context of manufacturing organizations. Before leaving the topic, it is worthwhile noting that just as industrial America has been reluctant to accept the customer as king, the health care industry has been averse to recognizing the patient as a customer with similar demands for quality, service, and competence. Historically, as patients we have depended on medical practitioners and institutions, often overlooking their shortcomings and excusing their arrogance. We value our health and well-being. Our relationships with physicians, nurses, and hospitals have usually been in critical and often life-threatening circumstances. It's not surprising that we have acquiesced to performances and practices often less-than-hoped-for or expected, and to relationships sometimes dehumanizing.

Today, the competitive realities of the health care industry include the staggering costs of rapidly advancing technologies, liability insurance and litigation, and professional specialty education. State and federal governments are now involved; patients and their employers are speaking up.

33

Fortunately, or really unfortunately, patients have gained more attention and priority only by the blatant intrusion of these external realities and their vested interests.

Like some industrial organizations, certain creative health care organizations have led the way in visualizing and addressing the need for change in favor of the customer. There have also been individual leaders, of whom Dr. Mitchell T. Rabkin, president of Beth Israel Hospital in Boston for over twenty-five years, has perhaps been the most conspicuous. As early as 1972, he recognized the organizational imperatives underlying patients' demands and the likelihood that Beth Israel Hospital's referring doctors would send patients to alternative hospital services, particularly in Boston's sophisticated medical health care marketplace. With unique foresight and conviction, Dr. Rabkin developed the official statement of a "Bill of Rights" for patients at Beth Israel Hospital in Boston. With Dr. Rabkin's permission, I quote just the captions:

1. You have the right to receive the best care medically indicated for your problem, regardless of your race, color, religion, national origin, or the source of payment for your care.
2. You have the right to be treated respectfully by others, and to be addressed by your proper name and without undue familiarity.
3. You have the right to privacy.
4. You have the right to seek and receive all the information necessary for you to understand your medical situation.
5. You have the right to know when students are to perform specific examinations or treatments that pertain to your care.
6. You have the right to full explanation of any research study in which you may be asked to participate.
7. You have the right to leave the hospital even if your doctors advise against it, unless you have certain infectious diseases which may influence the health of others, or if you are incapable of maintaining your own safety, as defined by law.
8. By Massachusetts law you have the right of access to your medical record.
9. You have the right to inquire about the possibility of financial aid to help you in the payment of hospital bills and the right to receive information and assistance in securing such aid.

10. We believe you are entitled to know whether any facilities recommended for your use are businesses in which those making such recommendations have a significant financial interest, such as nursing homes, pharmacies, or laboratories.
11. You have the right not to be exposed to the smoking of others.

As fundamental as these statements are for the patients' rights, Dr. Rabkin also recognizes the patients' responsibilities to the attending medical practitioners and the hospital staff members:

> You also have some responsibilities. . . . Please be on time for scheduled appointments, or telephone the hospital when you cannot be. Bring with you information about past illnesses, hospitalizations, medications, and other matters relating to your health. Be open and honest with us about instructions you receive concerning your health; let us know immediately if you do not understand them or if you feel that the instructions are such that you cannot follow them.
>
> You have the responsibility to be considerate of other patients, and to see that your visitors are considerate as well, particularly with regard to noise and smoking. Because Beth Israel is a smoke-free hospital, you and your visitors must refrain from smoking.
>
> You also have a responsibility to be prompt about payment of hospital bills, to provide information necessary for insurance processing of your bills, and to be prompt about asking questions you may have concerning your bills.
>
> This message reflects the interest and philosophy of the entire staff of Beth Israel Hospital.
>
> Mitchell T. Rabkin, MD
> President

Dr. Rabkin's contribution to identity at Beth Israel Hospital determined, defined, and articulated the right job for Beth Israel Hospital and the criteria for doing the job right. Equally important was the implication that past performances, practices, and relationships had become inappropriate, inadequate, and in fact obsolete.

Dr. Rabkin's early initiatives provided the foundation upon which Beth Israel has developed its widely recognized Primary Care Process of Nursing, and more recently its institution-wide participative management process, PREPARE/21—PREPARING for the 21st Century.

Participation
Responsibility
Education
Productivity
Accountability
Recognition
Excellence

Beth Israel's current program is no accident, having slowly evolved over the course of twenty years under the guidance of several leaders at the hospital. I'd like to quote Rosabeth Moss Kanter's reminder (*Harvard Business Review*, July-August 1991):

> Xerox, Motorola, and Corning are considered exemplars of United States companies that have rethought their business models and renewed their organizations. Generally neglected in the accounts of successful change processes, however, is just how long it took each company to hit upon its approach and how much trial and error was involved. Corning began its partnerships five decades ago; Motorola had a participative management program in the 1970s; Xerox's companywide quality effort grew out of shaky and controversial attempts to promote employees' involvement and benchmarking a dozen years ago.

Beth Israel Hospital's experience affirms Kanter's observation. Their current PREPARE/21 process began in 1972 with the Patients Bill of Rights; Motorola's program began with their PMP (Participative Management Program) in the 1970s. Having been involved in the development of both programs, I have seen them evolve and implement the sequential principles and processes presented in this book. Their programs are not quick fixes but classic examples of fidelity to basic principles and creative servant leadership.

At both Motorola and Beth Israel Hospital, the leader has been perceived as the best means available to get employees where they need to go at a particular time. This process requires the leader to take an active, conspicuous role in developing a functional, not a hierarchical, relationship with employees. The storytelling leader personally develops and shares a professionally planned position, with credible relevance to employees. The leader is omnipresent in presenting the vision throughout the organization; he seems to be omniscient in describing the competitive realities facing the organization; and he never appears omnipotent regarding the means of achieving the changes required. That possibility and challenged potential is left to the followers in an organization. The leader is committed to enabling employees to achieve their personal, professional, and organizational objectives as responsible and committed members of the organization.

The leader-as-educator should consider four goals. The first is for all employees to *know* reality accurately and meaningfully. Second, employees must *understand* the facts—their sources, their validity, and their reliability—and have the opportunity to challenge their relevance. Understanding is not the same as knowing; understanding must follow knowing. The third goal is for employees to *comprehend* the consequences of these facts for themselves, for their company, and often for their industry and community. Employees must genuinely evaluate and comprehend negative as well as positive predictable consequences. Consequences must not be left to private conjecture or easy dismissal, but must be personally and organizationally manifested. The fourth goal is to gain personal *acceptance* of these facts of organizational life as relevant givens.

I talk about Donnelly like that, its openness in terms of its incredible trust-filled environment. It doesn't mean that Donnelly doesn't have terrible problems, but at the same time I feel there is always something you can do about it. I never feel powerless at Donnelly.

—Kay, systems development, Donnelly Corp.

A Definition of Leaders

Members of organizations should be able to perceive their leaders, whether as educators or as servants, as the *best means available*. This is a somewhat pragmatic definition of leadership, but these three words emphasize the importance of competitive realities in the life of an organization. Employees are always seeking, demanding the *best* in leadership, whether in corporate officers, union officers, or elsewhere. We think of competent leaders as the *means* to enable us to make a difference in surviving and in achieving success. Thinking of leadership as a means requires the leader to serve the organization, an idea echoing the title of

Robert Greenleaf's important book *Servant Leadership*, which convincingly documents a leader's opportunity and responsibility to serve.

A leader must be perceived as the best means; not anybody or everybody will suffice. In any competitive situation, there is always another contender waiting to capitalize on any personal or professional weakness. A leader and contenders for leadership should never forget that the dynamic situation—the organization's competitive reality—is a codeterminant of the leadership. The current reality provides a demanding opportunity and a timely responsibility for a leader to earn, demonstrate, and exercise his title. The accessibility or availability of the best means can become an essential personal and professional commitment with conspicuous priority. The leadership of Mr. Houghton of Corning and Mr. Booth of Polaroid demonstrated these qualifications. These gentlemen admitted that their personal presence was demanding, even tiring. Genuine leadership cannot be successfully delegated, whether in an industrial organization, a family, or a political office.

The first thing that impressed me prior to that was the first Christmas I was here. Dwane Baumgardner, the president, was walking around wishing everyone a merry Christmas, and I was working over at Third Street at the time. I asked him a question about the job I was on, "Why was it being run?" He sat down for about twenty-five minutes and explained it to me. Diagrammed it out. He said at the time they were willing to initially take a loss just to get into the market. The president of the company sat down with me and explained it and that really impressed me.

—Don, line auditor, Donnelly Corp.

Another part of my definition of leadership is the focus on *this particular time*. This feature suggests a dynamic quality for the conditions, time, and performance demands that allow us to view the idea of mere renewal with skepticism, and accept the fact that change is our only hope. An understanding of the currency and urgency of reality is an essential part of organizational literacy. Today many organizations, even entire industries, and especially their employees, are severely disadvantaged because they become literate too late to change. Employees are left to wonder what happened, rather than having the opportunity to change and take charge of their own fates. No doubt many employees in the automotive industry woke up one morning with a feeling of futility and without a job.

We went for almost three years without paying a bonus. We had at the time, and any company will have during a very difficult time, layoffs and substantial reductions in employment. A lot of frustrations. A lot of feelings of insecurity. . . . At that time, I found participation made a major difference in the way we were able to dig out of that. We came out of the recession not as a weak and battered company that survived, but we really blasted right out of it. . . . The reason is that we had a lot of meetings with employees. We dealt with frustrations. We identified them. We used participation a great deal. We developed plans. We called them "recession response" plans that were developed in a participative environment. That led to relatively high levels of understanding, support, and commitment for the actions that had to be done or taken at the time.

—*Dwane, president, Donnelly Corp.*

And so we come to a disarmingly simple definition of leadership in the context of the Frost-Scanlon process. *A leader is perceived by followers as the best means available of getting them where they need to go (from here to there) at that particular time.*

Union Leadership

In defining leadership in an organization the identity of the union leader must be recognized and capitalized upon from the beginning. The union president, no less than corporate executives, must develop into a true leader if the Frost-Scanlon process is to function and the organization is to survive and prosper. Because this union officer is elected by the local's constituents, he or she is perceived by the members as their best means available to get them where they need to go at this particular time. A union introduces two leaders into an organization, a state of affairs that need not be problematic and may even help the organization toward effectiveness (doing the right job) and efficiency (doing the job right). We should ask some questions. Do the two leaders contradict each other? Accepting the union as a legitimate given in many companies, how can organizations capitalize upon the presence, purposes, and potentials of union leadership? In forty years of consulting, I have never seen an organization decertify its union or a union organize previously nonunion employees. The presence or absence of a union may be one part of reality that is an organizational given. Roles and relationships, however, can change dramatically—to everyone's advantage.

We must pose the same questions to union officers and members that we have been asking of organizations at large. Is change their only hope? Is education their best investment in achieving change? Is there a local union story to tell? What were the original circumstances surrounding the organization of the local union? What are the achievements of the local union: its *performances* in wages, benefits, job security, and working conditions? Its *practices* in bargaining—strikes or concession? Its *relationships*—adversarial or cooperative? Telling the local union story of past performances, practices, and relationships should remind the employees of who they are, where they came from, why they are here, and how they got here. The story should describe the current situation and question the appropriateness of past performances, practices, and relationships in the light of the company's competitive situation. The local union storyteller must be informed, articulate, trustworthy, and credible. Inasmuch as the union president is elected, he, like the Nigerian tribal elders, has an inherent responsibility to educate people as to the relevance of past, present, and future reality.

After a lot of finger pointing, we decided to try Scanlon [at Neelon Castings, Ltd.]. We saw for the first time the real chance to share in the equity, the company's profits. But you have got to trust the integrity of management before the union can ever agree to this style of management. Let's face it, up to now, unions have been fearful of trying out this kind of thing. There's been a lot of abuse on both sides that has made us feel this way. But it is a new day. We all have to find better ways of doing things if we are going to stay competitive in the world.
—Simon, United Steelworkers of Canada regional rep.

The local union president is the most logical person to tell the company's local union story. Is the story different than the company president's story? Should both stories be told? Should there be two storytellers? Should all employees hear both the union and the company stories? Should the stories be told at the same occasion? Or should the union story be told at the Union Hall, the customary site? It has been my experience that the autonomy of the union is appropriate and is strengthened by early and independent storytelling. Still, the same critical questions face both company and union. Are the local union's past performances, practices, and relationships now inappropriate, or even obsolete, in light of the current competitive realities? The union president must obtain the membership's approval to explore further with the organization the need to change.

In my experience, attendance at local union meetings is variable and usually minimum except in emergencies. It is entirely appropriate for the company president to announce officially and conspicuously that, consistent with the company's recognition and honoring of the contractual relationship with the local union, members are expected to attend union meetings simply to be informed. If local union members are to make a decision, the company president can request them, once fully informed, to take action in the best interests of themselves and their company. The maturing organization will be genuinely advantaged by such collaboration between the local union leadership and the company leader.

It should be clear that the company president has the singular responsibility of telling the company's story—past, present, and future. That story includes, comprehensively, the customer/marketplace, the physical resources of facilities, the equipment and technology, the financial resources, and the human resources. The union president is qualified and responsible for telling the local union's company story. Inasmuch as the union president has been typically concerned with the human resources, performances, practices, and relationships, it is appropriate and usually helpful for the company leader to call on the union president for studied observations and statements relevant to the challenging question of whether there is a compelling need for change. In answering this question, the respective identities and responsibilities of the company president and the local union president should become clear and functional, and leave no room for confusion or compromise. At the same time, this procedure affirms the president's integrity through his recognizing the contractual relationship.

The collaboration between company leader and union leader in the telling of organizational stories demonstrates the real and mutual position of all employees in the company. It also defines and demonstrates the legitimate differences in the roles and responsibilities of the company president and the local union president. The consequences of choosing change—the only real choice, I would argue—should be made crystal

41

clear to the local union membership and to all employees. The decision to change is an opportunity that only management leadership can offer. The possibilities then become infinite.

I know at times, when we've had representatives from Akron (corporate headquarters) down, they were surprised at the knowledge that the employees had of Firestone. We knew more about it; we knew what the money was. We knew what it cost to do this, and we knew how much money we were making. And, so I think it brought us closer to management and changed it from the standpoint that we felt closer and were a more closely knit part of Firestone than just employees making a living.

—*Don, machine tool operator, Firestone Tire*

Organizational Mandate

A lucid organizational mandate is a sure sign of a servant leader building identity and working at education. The mandate is not the statement of the chief executive officer's wish list, his personal philosophy, or the organization's philosophy. The mandate is defined and *dictated* by the organization's external realities, which are imperative and not personally selected options. A mandate differs from a mission statement, goals, and objectives. The mandate focuses on, and is limited to, four factors that are the total comprehensive province of management. This small number of factors belies the common opinion that management must always deal with multiple factors; it does not mean that formulating a mandate is easy. The factors are: the customer—consumer, end-user, client, patient, or student; physical resources represented by facilities, equipment, technology, systems, and supporting infrastructures; financial resources; and human resources.

The word *mandate* implies undeniable expectations in managing these four resources. These expectations originate outside the organization, and yet they belong to every member of the organization. To educate employees about their relationship to external realities—to raise an organization's literacy—the leader's best educational tool, one that tells a credible and convincing story, is the mandate. The development of an organization's mandate is a uniquely personal opportunity and responsibility of the leader and a test of leadership. The experience has proved to be an unexpectedly challenging assignment for chief executive officers in becoming genuine servant leaders.

Hugh DePree developed the following mandate for Herman Miller, Inc. It provides creative guidelines, which at first reading may seem very general in principle and practice. The imperative is expressed in the first paragraph: "Herman Miller must be an international organization in which people define and solve problems." Herman Miller is not to be a volume-market, commodity-oriented company, at least not in 1979. The first paragraph also dictates "products and services which improve the quality of life in the *working* and *healing* environments," specifically not in the residential environment. This paragraph dictates the right job. The commitment to performance, practices, and relationships is stated in paragraph three: "We are committed to quality and excellence in all that we do and the way in which we do it." Here is the mandate in full.

The Herman Miller Mandate

Herman Miller must be an international organization in which people define and solve problems. Problem definition, problem solving, through innovation wherever possible, must result in products and service which improve the quality of life in the working and healing environments.

At Herman Miller, people do this through having the responsibility and opportunity to contribute, to participate, to be involved, to own the problem and, indeed, to own Herman Miller.

We are committed to quality and excellence in all that we do and the way in which we do it.

We seek to be socially responsible and we share a concern and responsibility for the quality of the environment in which we and our neighbors live and work.

Profit is an essential and enabling factor in all annual and long-range planning and operations. Specific profit goals will be set annually.

Growth is implicit but must come because of the quality of the problem solution and the potential in our people and our program.

Hugh DePree, President and Chief Executive Officer

Another mandate, this one developed by Tony Spuria for the Fairchild Burns Company identifies the four imperatives affecting the four factors of management's assignment:

Fairchild Burns Mandate

1. To solve the ever increasing problems of our customers by continually providing the highest quality airline seats and introducing new and better products. Otherwise, they will turn to our competition. Without customers and more customers there is not security for tomorrow.
2. To effectively manage our physical resources—facilities, equipment, supplies, materials, etc.—ensuring adequate returns on investment. Our corporate management and shareholders will continue to make cash available for capital expenditures, only if the return on investment is acceptable.
3. To ensure continued profitability—profits are a cost of doing business, not a reward for the few. To use capital in our business, we must first generate it.
4. To manage human resources—making our company the best employment opportunity in terms of return on our personal investment of energy, education, training, and expertise.

My commitment to these stated objectives is such that I consider them Fairchild Burns Company mandates. I hope you will also accept them as our company mandates and help to make those changes necessary to enable us to react to outside influences. This undoubtedly will result in better products than those offered by our competitors and a much improved quality of life for all of us.

A. J. Spuria

The personal and professional identity of A. J. Spuria as president of the company is clear and consistent with his challenge to the employees that "Fairchild is Where the Sky is Not the Limit."

The imperatives of the marketplace are established by the ruthless and relentless demands of customers for increasingly superior quality, unflagging service, and better prices. The imperative on physical resources is the unforgiving expectations of shareholders for higher and growing returns on their capital investments. The imperative on financial resources is to increase revenues and profits, which are essential in doing business both today and tomorrow. They are the source of cash flow, research, and advancing technologies. The imperative on human resources is that competence is always in short supply. To attract and retain the needed and most competent personnel is now not only a domestic, but a global challenge. The mandate is *the what* of the organization's objectives that must be achieved to satisfy essential investors—customers, shareholders, and employees. For example, Herman Miller must be an *international organization* in which people *define and solve problems* . . . and must result in products and services which *improve the quality of life* in *working and healing environments.*

The mandate acknowledges that people and forces outside the organization can, do, and will exercise their options. Customers have freedom in their response to suppliers' performances, products, and services. There is little, if any, brand loyalty; American customers have vigorously resisted nationalistic appeals. Customers have literally invaded vendors' workplaces, telling them what to do and how to do it. New developments in technology have placed heavy burdens on capital budgets. The financial market has been fickle and ruthless in its quarterly demands, influenced by conglomerate funds readily manipulated by systems whose sole purpose is to accumulate money for anonymous and uncommitted investors. The most competent employees have the freedom to play the field of employment opportunities. All four factors to be considered in a mandate are, in a sense, outside the control of the organization. Yet an organization is heavily dependent on them for success.

Owners, investors expect a return on their money. I can't think of a better way to do that than to have some kind of management plan that allows everyone to participate. Commitment breeds commitment. If the investor sees how much each worker is committed to the process, then he or she is going to commit their dollars. Let's face it, without the investor, we're all out of the ballgame.
—Dick, CEO, Herman Miller, Inc.

Once the leader has drafted a mandate addressing customers and physical, financial, and human resources, he convenes his immediate executive staff at a special occasion to share this draft with them as a working paper. He begins the meeting by telling the company story, which should clearly demonstrate the chronology of the past, present, and future. The story should highlight his personal, professional, and organizational relationship and relevance to the mandate. The leader commonly shares with his executive staff his personal reasons for coming to, remaining with, and leading the company. His professional reasons ought to be clear and relevant. Candid and believable motivations dramatically model the sincerity and integrity of a leader. They also challenge the executive staff to review what the right job is for them personally and professionally and the criteria for doing the job right. As important as these steps are, the ultimate value and payoff is the focused impact of the mandate on the leader's and the executives' ability to know, understand, comprehend, and accept change as the way to survival and success.

The processing of a mandate has proved to be an exciting experience for many leaders. When John Boettner had finished the story of inaugurating for the Firestone Corporation its entirely new operation in Wilson, North Carolina—his new assignment—he announced to his immediate staff that he had selected each of them from throughout the corporation as his first choice for the executive team. The response was dramatic, though silent, exultation at having been so personally and professionally recognized. One can only imagine the pride and also the great personal expectations entailed in accepting the challenge John Boettner expressed in his mandate.

In a sophisticated professional service organization, the leader revealed that he had been offered two nationally conspicuous professional appointments. The staff members were surprised to learn of these singular offers and even more surprised that he had not accepted either of them. One vice president admitted asking himself afterward, "Would his leader have taken him on the new assignment? And if not, just what would he do now?" The personal and professional storytelling assignment is the springboard for processing the organization's mandate with sincerity and personal integrity.

Defining and finalizing a mandate becomes an educational process in which a leader deliberately articulates and documents the right job for his company and the criteria now required to do that job right. If this statement is received as old hat or simply continues standard operating procedure, forget it! If the story is genuinely perceived as requiring change and the listeners truly believe that change is the only hope, then continue. The story must convince them that past performances, practices, and relationships, especially among themselves, are no longer appropriate. If there is no real interest in the story and no growing conviction of the need to change, stop here! If the leader notices his audience leaning into the wind, as it were, then he must present, document, and develop the evidence in each of the four areas that support the compelling reasons for change. The occasion should be open to, in fact begs for, challenges: "How come? Why now? Who says so? What evidence is there to go that far?" External evidence should substantiate the imperatives. The questions and challenges to the leader should reveal competence, insights, maturity, and commitment. The staff should introduce their respective professional data, experience, and judgments, significantly enhancing the discussions and evaluations. It should be a constructive experience in personal, professional, and organizational development.

Four Educational Steps

Four educational steps are appropriate and essential in finalizing a mandate. The executive leaders of the company need to *know* the mandate. They need to *understand* the evidence that led to the conclusions in the mandate and its relevance to the present and future. They should be the first to challenge underlying premises, unwritten assumptions, or conscious omissions. They thereby affirm their respective professional identities. They need to *comprehend* the consequences for themselves and the company of meeting or not meeting the challenges of the mandate. The evaluation of both the positive and the negative consequences provides the basis for the fourth step—the *acceptance or rejection* of this organizational mandate.

If the working-paper mandate is insufficient in any regard, then it is appropriate and essential for the leader to accept the valid inputs cordially and proceed to prepare another draft. The steps in the educational process must be deliberate and not hurried to accommodate the leader. Even though a personal statement from the leader, the mandate must be seen as an organizational instrument. If there seems to be general agreement, then it is time to ask for a confidential vote to accept the statement as the organization's basis for action. Political dynamics are always present, and the leader must know unequivocally, by *confidential* straw vote, if the executive staff accepts this statement. It is critical for the leader, but also for these peer executives, to know the results of the vote. With no consensus, the leader must decide either to abandon the process or to rework the instrument. If there is consensus, the leader can assume a baseline of organizational literacy.

Now, at this point it is appropriate to ask the logical question of the executive team: "Are you personally and professionally able and willing to fulfill the demands of the organizational mandate?" You might assume that after such a rigorous process, affirmative answers would be a fore-gone conclusion. The novelty and dynamics of the situation should alert you to such naiveté, however. To the contrary, the rigorous experience should stimulate the following questions among the executive team:

> Do I need this company?
> Does the company need me?
> Are past performances, practices, and relationships now inadequate and inappropriate?
> What are the specific implications of these findings on the individual members—personally and professionally?
> Is change my only hope?

The two qualities of ability and willingness must be separated to reach the right personal and professional decisions. It is appropriate for the executives to ask, explore, and determine whether this company provides the best employment opportunity. What are the alternatives? Are we able to change? Willing to change? What is in it for us? Is there enough in it for us to change? When executives sincerely reflect on these questions over an appropriate period of time and responsibly answer them, some members may decide to leave or request reassignment within the organization.

My experience suggests that the leader make it clear that competitive realities demand changes of everyone, that there are personal and professional questions now about their ability and willingness to change. The answers will eventually become a matter of public record, documented by subsequent behavior. At this point in the process, the responses to the leader should be confidential. The leader needs to know if these key organizational leaders buy in and own the problem, and if they accept the challenge to change personally and professionally in meeting the mandate. Even though it is surprising, and at times even shocking, when a colleague quietly decides to terminate his relationship with the group and the organization, the decision must be respectfully accepted. That decision not only substantiates the process of personal and organizational development, but it introduces its own agenda for personal and professional integrity.

The final step in enabling the executive staff to become totally literate regarding the mandate is conducted at a specially arranged session. The members are requested to prepare, in detailed, written form, the personal and professional competencies, contributions, and commitments they are able and willing to make to assure the achievement of the mandate. As they share with the group their prepared statements at the special session, they open themselves to questions and to challenges as to the appropriateness, timeliness, and adequacies of their inputs, as well as their criteria, interdependencies, degrees of confidence, and benchmarks. It is a rigorous examination for every member and a novel experience for most executives. It is a genuine peer review, essential if this group is to pursue the mandate's demands vigorously and confidently. At the completion of the exchanges, the leader announces that *now* they know, understand, comprehend, and accept the organization's mandate; *now* they have declared their ability and willingness to own the mandate; and *now* they have evaluated the competencies, contributions, and commitments of their immediate colleagues (an essential level of literacy). A final confidential straw vote will affirm or deny that they believe *this* executive team can meet the challenges of the organization's mandate. Now is the time and occasion to accept or reject the responsibility to influence corporate decisions in their respective areas of competence.

Every time you're given a freedom, you're also given a responsibility. You have to do your homework. You don't just go up there and cry and whine and come up with some half-cocked idea. You've got to do your homework. But you're given the opportunity to do that.

—*Pat, production coordinator, Herman Miller, Inc.*

A less-than-unanimous vote means that the leader must take more time to build the right team or abandon the process for the moment. Split votes are not uncommon. Only unanimous approval completes the first step in enabling the organization to become literate and accept change as the only hope. Then, and only then, can the educational process of identifying organizational realities begin to enter the organization echelon by echelon. Since the leader is perceived by followers as the best means available for getting followers where they need to go at a particular time, the company president is an indispensable teller of the story. In fact, after all of the preparations just described, the author of the mandate is usually anxious to take on the demanding, sometimes awesome, assignment of telling the story to the entire organization. It is a lifetime career investment that I encourage a leader to make, an investment allowing a leader to become someone or something he or she never was before. When a

49

genuine and long-lasting commitment is to be offered, surrogates are not appropriate. Leader and followers need to know, look each other in the eye, and exchange lifelong IOUs. A most telling conclusion to Beth Israel's story was Dr. Rabkin's or David Dolin's question: "What will keep you at Beth Israel the next ten years?" The question evoked genuine and sober reflection, and then sometimes fantastic pledges of mutual commitment *IF* the direction and momentum for change, excellence, and competence were pursued.

A Quiz You Cannot Fail

To document and reinforce fidelity and integrity, I strongly recommended that the leader request confidential feedback from employees at the end of each session by asking the following questions:

1. Have I convinced you that there are compelling reasons to change? (Answer: yes or no)
2. Are there genuine opportunities to improve? (Answer: yes or no)
3. What is in it for you? (Or, is there enough in it for you to change?) Write down three or four reasons for you.
4. Are you willing to elect an ad hoc committee to work with management in developing a change process for our organization? (Answer: yes or no).

I suggest that the security of the confidential vote be assured by a joint employee and management committee to count the votes only after all employees have voted. To speak to all employees and allow them to vote may require several days in larger companies. Take a vote at the end of each meeting, when the facts have just been presented and openly challenged, and attention is most focused on the organizational message. This will avoid distortions of the evidence for the mandate and will focus the group on the present and future, rather than on the hang-ups of the past. The process will establish personal trust and commitment between a leader and employees, and will set the expected protocol for future meetings.

Based on my experience, I suggest that only a 90 percent affirmative vote be accepted as proof of a literate and willing commitment. If 90 percent of employees *know* their company's competitive realities, *understand* the data supporting the facts, *comprehend* the personal and organizational consequences of those realities, and *accept* personally and professionally the opportunity and responsibility for effecting the mandated changes, the organization is sufficiently literate to proceed. This entire process then becomes a public statement of mutual fidelity toward establishing and authenticating the integrity of the organization in all of its relationships to customers, investors, and employees.

It is important to caution clearly that the purpose of the vote is not to give the employees the opportunity and responsibility to decide whether the organization is or is not going to explore a new agenda. The confidential vote is a genuine opportunity to *influence* the leader's decision. Employees must first decide if they are able and willing to accept the responsibility of voting confidentially to influence the leader's decision. The leader needs to know how many employees are convinced by his story of the need to change, believe changes are possible, consider change worth their while, and are willing to become involved. The leader needs to know if the percentage is 10, 24, 51, or 90. With that data, a leader can make the best decision on behalf of the organization. The wisdom of a competent leader will determine whether to pursue organizational change or abandon the exploration at this point. The leader can never delegate the responsibility to decide.

What can happen in an organization in which 90 percent are literate and have publicly declared their personal, professional, and organizational ability and willingness to change? Only then are employees qualified to consider the second principle in the Frost-Scanlon process. It may seem that I have belabored the principle of identity, the process of education, and the goal of employee literacy. Yet companies such as Motorola, Herman Miller, and the Donnelly Corporation have proved that the succeeding principles and processes are built on, and absolutely depend on, the literacy of the entire organization about its identity. As Paul Kalkman, former President of the Donnelly Corporation, insists, "They must first pass the reality check." As Sandra Kirsch reminds us in *Fortune* (3 June 1991):

> Brainpower has always been an essential asset. It is, after all, why *Homo sapiens* rule the roost. But it has never before been so important for business. Every company depends increasingly on knowledge—patents, processes, management skills, technologies, information about customers and suppliers, and old-fashioned experience. Added together, this knowledge is intellectual capital . . . . In other words, it's the sum of everything everybody in your company knows that gives you a competitive edge in the marketplace.

I like to hear them say, "Yes, we're going to be breaking into the Japanese market." Having to increase production from what we have, fifty percent . . . I look forward to the challenge. I look forward to the opportunity to have to do that. That I can get a machine to run so good that it is running every day. I know that we are going to make the parts then. We're going to sell them.

—Dave, maintenance electrician, Donnelly Corp.

The Process of Education

In 1976, *Harvard Business Review* staff members interviewed Mr. John Fenlon Donnelly, the venerated storyteller of the Donnelly Corporation. I believe the questions posed to Mr. Donnelly and his responses are especially relevant in capturing the spirit of the need for a leader's openness to the talents of others in serving the organization:

HBR: People often like the sound of industrial democracy, and yet it hasn't taken hold very fast in the United States. Why do you think people are skeptical about approaches like Donnelly's?

MR. DONNELLY: They're afraid of losing authority.

HBR: Why do you think they believe authority works better?

MR. DONNELLY: Because that's the way it's been done, and that's the way organizations are structured. They're mostly modeled after the military, and it's difficult for people to conceive of any other system working. I would be the last one to say that we don't use authority in this company. We do. But, to the extent that you have to rely on the authority of your position, you're a questionable manager. If you are not in the position to get people to accept ideas because they're sound and if you are not willing to accept an idea because it's sound, then you're really not a good manager.

So it's not a matter of throwing positions of authority but of playing them down. That's difficult for people to do. It's an unknown world. The first time you really stick your neck out to make it work, you see that it's a risk. You can look awfully silly if you stick your neck out and people don't respond. The first few times you stick your neck out, people may not respond. They may say, "What kind of stuff is this?" So until people have models that they can see are successful, it's going to be quite hard. More and more companies are finding that to continue to operate they have to have better contact with all their people. You have to stop the alienation. And you don't stop that except by getting at the root causes of alienation. (*Harvard Business Review* Jan-Feb, 1977, 117-27)

It may be worthwhile to compare the leadership process in the academic educational setting to that in the industrial or service company context. Sound pedagogy requires the teacher to ascertain what, if anything, was learned. Remember that teaching centers on the teacher; learning resides in students. A great many teachers teach students who learn very little. (Many employees, like students who drop out, find their work situations intellectually and personally frustrating and uninteresting.) Regardless of who is to blame, the desired result is not achieved. Oral and written examinations are wholesome and essential ways for the teacher to discover how effective his or her *teaching* is at motivating a student to *learn*. In organizations, the leader (executive, manager, or supervisor) often assumes that he or she has been an effective teacher of the reality facts and that employees have understood them—have *learned*. We assume that managers and executives are well paid to know and to communicate the answers; it is unnecessary to find out whether the rank and file have learned anything. Nothing could be further from the truth. These assumptions only foster false confidence in the leader and suggest an arrogance of omniscience. A servant leader will do whatever it takes to help people learn. In a paradoxical way, teaching becomes irrelevant when learning is the goal.

I have a responsibility to make sure that the opinions of everyone are at least solicited when I am after information, or someone else is after information. This is a conscious effort on my part, to make sure that they have an opportunity to speak.

—Jim, manufacturing and engineering group, Donnelly

What would occur if, after a leader had presented an exciting and demanding competitive update, he asked the simple question, "Have I convinced you that there are compelling reasons to change? To improve? To go for perfection? To move from two sigma to six sigma of quality performance? Just write down your answer—yes or no." From my experience, these questions will take people by surprise. The leader should caution the members not to answer "yes" automatically. The leader should tell them that "if I have not convinced you, tell me so, and I will go and get better data, or even bring in the customer to tell the story." Would this feedback process help to improve the leader's teaching skills and enable the employees to learn and change more efficiently? From my experience, it has proved to be a mutually rewarding exchange.

So every month, improvements, problems, and so on are brought back before the whole plant. So areas that might not even know what the calendar machine does are aware of what they do and the problems they have. I think this plantwide idea has worked very well. . . . This attitude has greatly helped—just education!
—*Carol, process engineering, Firestone Tire*

Go a step further. Inasmuch as organizational settings are freighted with political worries, I suggest that confidential votes will assure more reliable feedback and avoid political pressure not to make waves. For example, in a sophisticated service organization, after the executive had presented a revealing story of the competitive need to change, a confidential vote was taken. According to the count, three out of twenty-five staff members were not convinced of the need to change or improve. When the vote was announced to the group, the highly respected and competent executive spontaneously and emotionally expressed disbelief that he had not convinced *every* member of that group of the need to change. He immediately asked, "What could I tell you or do to convince you who voted negatively?" He was quickly reminded that the vote was confidential. Slightly chagrined, he graciously withdrew his request. He added, "If anyone would like to write me anonymously in the next few days, I will be reading my mail." This officer is competent, highly respected, and even loved by these staff members. He is becoming a better teacher. His staff members are becoming promising and responsive students.

In my experience, too often executives or managers go to meetings, deliver reports and official statements, or make rounds in operating sites protected behind a mind-set of surveillance and omniscience. They are not open—nor are they motivated—to discover or learn something they never knew before. Some officers even think it incumbent upon them to appear to be "making the rounds." Remember that a leader must be perceived as a means. Followers will decide for themselves based upon what they see. Unfortunately, they are seldom given a real opportunity to evaluate a superior's ability and willingness to teach or to lead. If students or employees have not learned, it is clear they were not taught. The price of illiteracy is staggering and is paid by individuals, organizations, our country, and our culture. Thousands of employees in the steel, textile, and automotive industries are unemployed because they became competitively illiterate, both intellectually and in their skills. They were not taught and did not learn. They did not have the organizational opportunity to take the course and prepare for the final examination. The city of Flint, Michigan, is only one example, one well documented in the film "Roger and Me."

In summary, when the first principle of the Scanlon process, identity, has been implemented by an effective and efficient process of education conducted by a true servant leader, a wonderful relationship arises and leads to personal, professional, and organizational growth and improvement. Literacy, the foundation for identity and the goal of education, begins with the definition and articulation of the right job and the competitive criteria for doing that job right. Literate employees can then see that past performances, practices, and relationships are inappropriate; that present competitive realities require change; and that future survival and success must be earned by becoming conspicuously unique in responding to customers' needs and demands.

You bet we can satisfy our customer. Why? Because we know what he wants from us. And we work together to make it happen.
—Vanderhill, supervisor, Herman Miller, Inc.

Summary: Principle of Identity and Process of Education

The following chart summarizes the principle of Identity and the process of Education. The goal is organizational and personal literacy.

Identity: Personal, Professional, Organizational

A. What is the right job (effectiveness)?
   What are the criteria for doing the job right (efficiency)?
B. Are past performances, practices, and relationships adequate? appropriate? obsolete?
   Are present competitive realities compelling reasons to change?
   Do future survival and success require earning unique identities as perceived and experienced by customers, investors, and employees?
C. Is change the only hope?
D. Is education the most promising instrument?
E. Is the leader perceived by the followers as the best means available to get them where they need to go at this particular time?
F. Mandate development—chief executive officer as servant leader
   External imperatives: customers/marketplace; physical resources/capital investors/ROI; financial resources/fiscal support; human resources
G. Processing the mandate with executive managers
   1) Know the mandate
      Understand the mandate
      Comprehend the mandate
      Accept the mandate
   2) Ability and willingness to change to achieve mandate
   3) Commitment to the executive team as competent and committed
H. Education of entire company membership, echelon by echelon

I. ***Final Examination: A Quiz You Cannot Fail***
   Are you convinced there are compelling reasons for you and the organization to change?
   Are there genuine opportunities for you and the organization to improve?
   What is in it for you if you change?
   Are you willing to elect an ad hoc committee to work with management in developing a proposal for our company?

CHAPTER THREE

THE SECOND PRINCIPLE: PARTICIPATION

Definition

By requesting feedback during the introduction of the mandate, the leader has begun to demonstrate to employees the second principle of the Frost-Scanlon process: participation is the opportunity that only management can provide, and the responsibility that only employees can accept, to influence decisions in areas of one's competence. Opportunity like the one to vote confidentially on the mandate is, or should be, a mutually advantageous experience. The combination of opportunity and responsibility should not be left to chance. Management must create the occasion and tell the story, thereby affording the opportunity for employees to become literate. Employees must be challenged to know the reality, understand its bases, comprehend its implications, and accept the opportunity to become responsible. Without acceptance of the offer, the participative process is aborted. When people accept the opportunity to become responsible, they give the first sign of literacy, of recognizing the need to learn and to change. Giving opportunity and accepting responsibility demonstrate sharing and cooperation, rather than acts of demarcation and exclusivity.

It is part of the turf—it is the expectation to participate, both myself and my work team at all levels.

—Kelly, supervisor, Herman Miller, Inc.

Participation, as I see it, includes influencing decisions. Employees do not make all decisions; corporate decisions are management's responsibility. As Max DePree of Herman Miller puts it, participation means having a say, not having a vote. It's to everyone's advantage, however, to put all employees in a position to be heard and to make a difference in the quality of decisions. The responsibility of employees to influence decisions may well be a dramatic change in attitude for many organizations. Employees generally are not very skilled or practiced in the art of influencing decision makers, and managers are not very skilled or practiced in the art of listening and being influenced by subordinates. It should be made abundantly clear to the entire organization that the 90 percent majority affirmative straw vote was a genuine, participative act that did influence the leader. No matter how the vote is split, the leader should make it perfectly clear that the vote influenced his final decision, and how it did so.

Participation is the ability to give the input. At least you're given the opportunity to give your input, and it is listened to, but that does not necessarily mean it's followed.

—*Keith, molding machine operator, Donnelly Corp.*

The processes of education and accepting of responsibility demonstrate and confirm to employees that they are not being asked, or expected, to do more than they are competent to do. However, these processes should also convince the organization that current competencies are not going to be sufficient to meet changing competitive demands.

As education is the process that accomplishes literacy, acceptance of ownership is the process that accomplishes participation. Participation is basic to one of our cherished American dreams—an ownership stake in the enterprises to which we contribute our talents and our work. Without the opportunity to own a piece of the action and to become responsible for their own performances, practices, and relationships in achieving corporate objectives, employees become renters, irresponsible occupants, without the attachment to a home in which they have some equity. Employees without ownership are merely "job renters," an economic and social drain we cannot afford. Truly, ownership is a competitive necessity today.

No one is making you learn, making you memorize this information. You have to listen. Being willing to speak up on things that I think I have significant information ought to be considered when decisions are being made. Being willing to make decisions. Being willing to support people to make decisions, whether they are part of my work team or not. Being willing to ask people why decisions are made in the way they are. All of these things influence decisions that are going on.

—Jim, manufacturing and engineering group, Donnelly Corp.

Ownership can be offered and implemented in many ingenious ways. Employees in participative companies have accepted the opportunity to visit with prospective and current customers in evaluating their specific needs, causes of dissatisfaction, and expectations. When the Herman Miller employees at Prairie Junction, Texas, learned that their new neighbor was going to be the American Airlines national office, they sent a personal letter requesting that the airline give serious consideration to Herman Miller's furniture for this new facility. It resulted in a significant order. When the installation was ready for the official opening, the employees on their own time and initiative went to check the installation. They discovered that the packing crates had depressed the plush on the chair fabrics. There was only a weekend before the Monday grand opening. The employees—on their own time, around the clock—took steam irons to lift the plush on hundreds and hundreds of chairs. Perfection and customer satisfaction were their responsibility. After all, *their* company's reputation (all full-time employees own stock and receive profit sharing and bonuses) was on the line.

Opportunity and Responsibility

Management needs to develop the skills to provide the opportunities as well as to establish the process whereby the employees can accept responsibility and own the problem. History is replete with precedents, litigations, regulations, and contracts that have specifically inhibited or prevented the process of participation—giving, sharing, and taking. These past practices and their inherent adversarial relationships are inappropriate—truly obsolete.

Figure 3. Herman Miller, Inc. Advertisement

Knowing gives them a sense of ownership to the point where this one person said "If I wasn't important, why would they spend the time telling me that our accounts receivable are up and asking me to help? There's a reason they're telling me this." People can sense the ownership, so that they say, "Let's work harder," for example, "on making that product. Let's make it right so that the customer doesn't make a complaint and pays the bill on time." They can follow the whole thing down to the bottom line.

—Steve, production supervisor, Herman Miller, Inc.

When the employees of a Donnelly Corporation product division were frustrated by a customer's constant rejection of their product, in spite of their all-out efforts to satisfy them, three production employees at their own request drove four hundred miles to see for themselves. They discovered, among other things, that the customer was offering to its employees an incentive bonus for identifying less-than-perfect parts received from Donnelly. What an insidious challenge! The Donnelly employees had been given the opportunity to become personally literate, and they took it, educating themselves as to reality. Then they accepted the responsibility for solving the problem by producing perfect parts to satisfy their customer. There was no longer confusion, but an ownership of the demand for perfection.

As Kermit Campbell, former chief executive officer of Herman Miller, might say, this opportunity "liberated the spirit of employees." The consequence of this liberating opportunity is responsible ownership. Contrary to the furniture industry standard of fifty acceptable final products out of sixty pieces produced, Herman Miller employees accepted the responsibility of producing fifty perfect products out of fifty sets of parts entered into production. There is no confusion about effective performance or efficient practices on the job. There is a clear and common goal of fidelity to the customers, to the investors, and to their own professional competencies—fifty good parts in and fifty good products out!

The principle may seem clear, but the process of becoming responsible and accepting ownership must be absolutely genuine and authenticated throughout the organization, especially the commitment to satisfy customers. For example, the prestigious marketing group in a large company conceived of a corporate commitment to each and every customer with the engaging phrase "I promise!" The specifics of the program were well thought out and delineated in great detail by the marketing department. The company made quality and service commitments that the competition at the time was unable or unwilling to deliver. The slogan "I promise!" fit in well with the company's values, reputation, and vision. But let me quote the president at the time: "We made a commitment on behalf of all employees." This was a clue that the program would fail. A true commitment cannot be made on behalf of anyone. The program, which should have become part of the company's way of doing business from then on, did not realize its potential. The marketing department failed to realize that it could not promise performance for other employees without educating them, giving them the opportunity to know, understand, and comprehend the reasons behind the commitment, and enlisting their own personal commitment to customers.

To me, by being in the Scanlon Plan, they are giving me permission, so to speak, to participate. Without their backing, I don't believe it could go over or work.
—*Roger, maintenance department, Firestone Tire*

Motorola employees have accepted both personal and professional responsibility for gaining the skills required to achieve six sigma of quality performance because they are literate about "what day it is," about what level of competence they need to survive. They have welcomed change. In a 1991 advertisement, Motorola states: "If you don't like surprises, you're living in the wrong century." Motorola's success depends on every employee becoming more competent in responding to customers' expectation of perfection and accepting surprises as a normal part of life.

Ad Hoc Committee Participation

One of the tried and true participative practices is the use of Ad Hoc Committees. Remember that the leader asked the entire organization, "Are you willing to elect an Ad Hoc Committee to work with management in developing a specific proposal for our company?" This question is an obvious test of employees' willingness to accept responsibility in becoming involved in the change process. Forty years ago, when employees suspected that management would trick employees and their unions into a binding commitment in the proposal development, the term ad hoc became a way to crack old and rigid prejudices. Inasmuch as few employees or employers remembered their high school Latin, the phrase set up an occasion to define the term and thereby the limits of risk in participation. Ad hoc described a one-time, one-purpose, one-situation committee, to be terminated after serving that specific purpose. When management offered employees the ad hoc opportunity to become involved in developing the program for the organization, the employees considered it safe enough to participate, suspending the old practices of adversarial turf protection. Though times have changed, the ad hoc process is still standard procedure at Motorola, where the process is officially and widely referred to as "Ad Hocary."

Inasmuch as this collaborative process is often a first-time experience and should therefore be introduced as a genuine change, the criteria for membership on the Ad Hoc Committee should be clearly set forth to assure the election of the most appropriate employee representatives. An essential and conspicuous qualification is trustworthiness. Another is proven competence in representing constituents, particularly members of an entire organization. Another quality is a reputation for fairness without compromising fidelity to one's own constituents. In a union-organized company, the official union stewards and officers must not automatically become members of the Ad Hoc Committee. The criteria for serving on the Ad Hoc Committee must be clearly differentiated from the criteria for serving as stewards and officers of the union local. Neither should union leaders automatically be excluded from the committee. In fact, I strongly recommended that the president of the union local and one other officer be ex officio members of the Ad Hoc Committee. This step prevents any suspicion that the Frost-Scanlon process is in any way an intrusion into the union contract. If anything, the Ad Hoc Committee should reaffirm the organization's integrity in honoring the contract.

At some time, the earlier the better, but not later than at the time of the confidential vote, it is appropriate and necessary to declare officially the relationship of the company and the union local as together they explore and develop the proposal for change in the company. The following statement has been widely accepted by different unions and managements to verify the contractual relationship and to clarify the intent and the processes of participative management in achieving the company's survival and success. I recommend including it in the proposal prepared by the Ad Hoc Committee, signed by the general manager and the local union president.

Scanlon Process Memorandum of Agreement

The Union does acknowledge and recognize that the Fairchild Burns Company has implemented a Scanlon Plan at its Winston-Salem based operation. The Union does fully recognize and understand that this Plan is a participatory program which affects and involves all employees, and which is designed to attain the maximum potential from the Company's physical, financial, and human resources.

63

Both parties, the Company and the Union, do mutually understand and agree that the Scanlon Plan is not a substitute for collective bargaining and is not subject to collective bargaining. It is further understood and agreed upon by both parties that the Scanlon Plan is related to the improvement of productivity, and that the Plan will not infringe upon the provisions of the Labor Agreement.

The Company and the Union do further acknowledge that the Scanlon Plan should serve as a mechanism to improve the coordination of both labor and management in developing, pursuing, and achieving common goals.

The document puts both union and management officers on record in this exploration and proposal. It stipulates that the process will not infringe on the formal union/management contract and its provisions. It excludes the program from collective bargaining and establishes the process in spirit and substance as a participative enterprise. Admittedly, there have been occasions, especially during the succession of new chief executive officers unfamiliar and not yet committed to the participative process, when the union members and employees wished the process were protected by a collective bargaining agreement. However, I believe that genuine participation is best assured by public commitment—personally, professionally, and organizationally—of all parties. Without that public commitment, no program of personal and organizational development will survive or flourish.

It should not be inferred that the Frost-Scanlon process has no impact on formal contractual relationships. The organizational change represented by the Frost-Scanlon process should support and even reinforce the union's responsibilities for the security and welfare of its members by greater literacy and involvement among its members. The change establishes management's expectation that union members be well informed and make prudent decisions in their own *and* the company's best interests. Management encourages employees to attend local union meetings and to elect leaders who will serve them and their company. The union leadership must act as well-informed, competent, and articulate servants of their constituents. Management and union officials should avoid compromising, or even appearing to compromise, their respective offices. Their roles and responsibilities should be seen as discrete; the relationship between union and company should be soundly established and apart from the Ad Hoc Committee's considerations.

Participation in Action: The Development of the Proposal

The elected and appointed members of the Ad Hoc Committee are certainly to be congratulated by the company leader and employees. They should be officially charged with developing a most innovative, serviceable instrument that establishes the processes required to achieve the company's mandate: education, ownership, and accountability. The work of the Ad Hoc Committee is delegated to the following subcommittees: Education, Participation, and Equity.

Education Committee

Education assures the organizational literacy of *all* members, including new recruits. Personal and organizational literacy is a competitive necessity in the broadest sense—past, present, and future. Education must become part and parcel of the organization's daily life. The Education Committee's job is to develop the specific processes that establish, assure, and monitor—

1. management's provision of the opportunity to participate;
2. employees' acceptance of the responsibility to own the problem;
3. the establishment of innovative, effective, and efficient methods of influencing corporate decisions;
4. the recognition of identities, competencies, contributions, and commitments of all the areas of the organization; and
5. the provision of an audit committee to review and evaluate progress after a year. (This feature signals employees that the proposal will need to be refined. In the best of worlds, a genuine refresher at the end of the first year and a confirmation vote to continue is a wholesome procedure. It is surprising how much more diligent management is in maintaining a program when a straw vote on continuing the program is scheduled after the first year.)

Several years ago the Ad Hoc Committee at Herman Miller requested that the entire organization have access to an annual strategic and operational calendar. The committee developed a one-year and a three-year calendar (see fig. 4) that showed the early months of planning and challenging, the following months of testing the company's readiness, the successive stages of implementation, and finally the integrated operations.

65

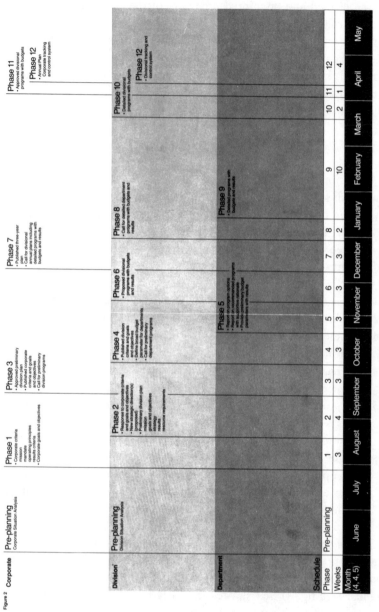

Figure 4. Herman Miller, Inc. Annual Planning Process

This calendar provided a real education for all employees about the many factors involved in research, developmental engineering, operational engineering and planning, and specification preparations. It helped correct some misinterpretations of actions and time lapses. More important, it provided an awareness of the many company functions and gave a rationality to time frames. The knowledge of the big picture allows employees the freedom to seek new and synergistic relationships, helping to reduce development time further and respond even more quickly to customers' requests. This illustration is an example that past practices can be changed in today's competitive world.

In conjunction with that program, the Education Committee at Herman Miller developed and introduced the "W" process of communication. The following diagram (see fig. 5) illustrates the fundamental steps of the participative process: providing the opportunities and accepting the responsibilities of determining and defining the right job (the what) and the criteria for doing the job right (the how).

The first leg of the "W" represents the "what" of competitive reality, provided by the executive echelon to the entire organization. The second leg of the "W" represents employees' challenges to the validity, reliability, and believability of the executive version of the facts. The third leg of the "W" represents the customers' criteria for doing the job right. The fourth leg represents employee feedback discussing how to meet these criteria

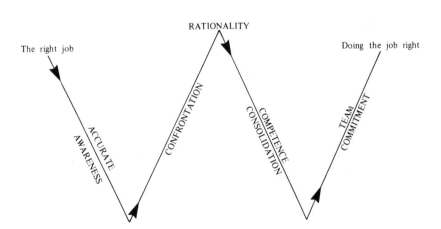

Figure 5. Process for Organizational Participation

and suggestions to improve quality, efficiency, or collaboration. The diagram lays out the relationships of leaders and followers, as well as the specific processes of providing the real opportunity to become literate, to accept responsibility. Moreover, it shows an established procedure for employees to influence decisions at the appropriate levels and in their areas of competence. The "W" format not only establishes the processes of education and ownership by transcending the hierarchy, but also serves as a prototype for education and ownership in divisions and departments. The supervisor of a department comprehends the corporate picture and shares it, along with specific information about "what" and "how," with his own departmental people.

Because it matters to the customers, to investors, to me—everybody—you're going to care about something you own. You get more involved.

—Don, upholsterer, Herman Miller, Inc.

The Work Team: Participation/Ownership Committee

To standardize and operationalize the Frost-Scanlon concept, the Ad Hoc Committee establishes the communication structure, the basic block of which is the work team. Every employee should be a member of a work team. The work team is the primary seat of identity in the company and the primary source of education about the compelling realities facing each work team. The work team leader has the responsibility for creating a rational working situation that recognizes the dignity of each member and challenges every member to help achieve the organization's mandate. The educational process is essential throughout the organization, even in areas where employees exercise considerable autonomy in specialized functions or services. Every employee must know "what day it is" every day. Special consideration for continuous education and involvement should be provided for every echelon and division where there is great diversity of professional members' sophistication and assignments. Medical doctors and researchers in health care institutions and professors, researchers, and administrators in academic institutions are good examples of people who need such consideration.

The educational experience in the work teams includes the assured opportunity to learn by being open to the challenges of "how come" and "why not." The work team agenda commonly focuses on customers' demands for superior quality of products and services, investors' demands for improving returns on their capital, and improving employees' competence in performance, practice, and relationships.

The work team is also the center of the representative process in organizations, a process well known in our democratic form of government. Work team members must have the opportunity to elect the person most competent and trustworthy to represent them. Competence and trustworthiness are as important and maybe more important in work situations than in our political system, where our choice of qualified candidates and our personal monitoring of their accountability in office is compromised by political parties and their processes. But in organizations, only assertive and faithful advocacy of constituents' needs combined with personal accountability will suffice to gain employees' and the organization's survival and success. The work team representative and hierarchical superiors are the key resources in establishing a rational and educational working environment for all members of an organization.

It makes me feel as though I am putting something into the company. It also gives me a lot more responsibility and a better feel of doing my job right. . . . It gives me a chance to be able to expand myself and grow. By management giving me this ability or trust, it makes me help myself along as well as the people working with me.

—Michael, production employee, Firestone Tire

A special feature of leadership should be clearly acknowledged in distinguishing between an elected and an appointed leader. The two roles should be apparent in the Ad Hoc Committee work, and they should be built into the participative education system. The appointed person derives authority and influence from the person appointing him or her. The elected leader derives authority and influence from constituents. The elected leader must never forget where he came from and to whom he is accountable. The organization must be aware of the origin and responsibility of these elected representatives and recognize these roles as unique company assets, even when elected leaders are at odds with appointed ones. Work team representatives provide unique sources of information, feedback, and challenge. Work teams represent the huge potential of literate, responsible, accountable, and committed employees.

I think the biggest way [to influence] is to just open my mouth. . . . When I ask questions, I'm influencing. My questions aren't always liked, but I guess I'm lucky. I never got one single repercussion from asking questions. If anything, I got advantages for asking questions.

—*Steve, production supervisor, Herman Miller*

Remembering that the process for operationalizing participation is ownership, education is the best way to convince employees of the compelling need for ownership. Ownership of the system of participation must also be enthusiastically accepted and diligently protected. The participative system must not be allowed to deteriorate to a perfunctory employee accommodation or be relegated to a human resources department. Such a condition is common. When it began to develop at the Ford Sharonville plant, the union officers staged an informal sit-down confrontation in the general manager's office to reinstate the participative process as a real priority for everyone. The meeting reminded managers and employees alike that employees must own the problem of quality assurance to customers. In that location, every departmental bulletin board affirms that every employee has the opportunity and responsibility to stop an operation when quality standards are not being adhered to. This experience illustrates the importance of employee ownership of the participative process. Only then do the rights of ownership come into play, establishing the legitimacy of possession and therefore of exercising, protecting, and defending these rights.

To be specific, the Ad Hoc Committee must establish conspicuous and reliable processes for every employee to become literate and to own the organization's future. Every employee should be able to relate his or her performance and contribution to (1) the organization's customers; (2) the organization's return on investments in equipment, facilities, and so on.; (3) the profitability of the organization; and (4) achieving the organization's objectives. These four areas of opportunity to know and to be involved are legitimate and should be the most frequent standard for problem ownership among supervisors and elected work team representatives. Using this standard, a corporate president was recently prompted to ask, "What do the one hundred-plus members of our legal staff contribute to our customers' assured satisfaction, company profitability, and corporate success?" The question proved to be a provocative challenge to ownership and gained both personal and professional responsiveness in sharpening employees' relationships with customers and with company identity.

As far as the investor is concerned, the employee has a stake in the company. I don't mean I have as big a stake as the person who owns shares in the company, but I have a stake in the company through participative management. When you say it's their money, it isn't. It is everybody's bonus.
—Don, line auditor, Donnelly Corp.

Participation: Colleges, Universities, Health Care Institutions

Before leaving the processes of education and ownership among all employees, I want to describe my experience with professional employees in hospitals and universities. In academic and medical settings, there seems to be a lack of interest among professional employees in any aggressive exploration into the organizational need to change, except as it might affect their personal or professional standing. These employees have shown little concern over the need to educate an entire organization about corporate change, to say nothing of acknowledging ownership of the problem. They don't seem to see the possibilities for improvement inherent in education and change. Their historic reward systems for research and independent practices have built and reinforced personal and professional identities, which are peripheral to the organization as well as being autonomous and self-governed. For example, with the large student bodies and historically generous public support of education, faculty have enjoyed the liberty to pursue their own interests. Research-granting agencies have been generous with them, and universities have competed vigorously for talented researchers. The work of the institution, its raison d'être—education of students—has been delegated to dedicated but inexperienced graduate students. There is seemingly little or no commitment asked for, or given, in fulfilling this institutional responsibility. (Our son Richard Frost has discussed this extensively in his doctoral dissertation, "An Investigation of Faculty Commitment to the University," Michigan

State University, 1991.) The accommodation of faculty members' research priorities by the institution's administrators has become a national scandal, as it involves government funding. Several leading universities have returned much grant money discovered to have been used for things other than research. This fiscal malfeasance suggests a predictable consequence of a flagrant denial or disregard of personal and professional identity and commitment to the institution's mandated priority: students' education and training.

In institutions officially committed to research, teaching, and health care delivery, a similar preoccupation with one's own career and practice has been tolerated and generally accepted as standard operating procedure for professional employees. The professional members of health care institutions are generally organizationally illiterate about external realities impacting our society, our political and economic systems, our communities, and specifically our citizens as their end users or customers. In spite of the origin and stated purposes of these institutions—teaching, research, and service—their professional members demonstrate little awareness of, concern for, or involvement in a public, mutual commitment to achieving the institution's mandate. Consequently, when an evaluative process for change is considered, professional employees find themselves confused as to the appropriateness of such an initiative and the relevance of the principles and processes to them. Because of their established and privileged positions, they resent intrusion and resist any involvement in change. The limited successes and common failures of programs for change in these institutions are due primarily to organizational illiteracy and personal infidelity to the opportunities to become responsible and accountable in fulfilling the institution's mandates. These professionals are too often renters rather than owners.

Leaders in health care and academic institutions have been unable or unwilling to turn the attention of these prestigious professional resources to the changed realities surrounding them. Specifically, what is the right job for their institutions today? In the state of Michigan, what is the right job for the University of Michigan in Ann Arbor, Wayne State University in Detroit, and Michigan State University in East Lansing, with its land grant origin and reputation? According to the *U.S. News and World Report* (30 September 1991), Williams College has been uniquely innovative and successful in not only addressing the question of what the right job is for Williams College today, but also how to do that job right as an academic institution. The college has met demographic changes in our society

72

head-on, strengthened its curriculum, and brought faculty and students together in all kinds of teaching and learning situations. Williams College has changed from a "preppy, small-school alternative to Harvard" to an institution dealing honestly with today's realities.

What is the right job for a hospital today? Is it a community hospital or a research-teaching-health care delivery hospital? Or is it like, the Mayo Clinic in Rochester, Minnesota, primarily clinically oriented and committed? What are their nationally attracted customers' needs? What are the fiscal realities of their technologically advanced and sophisticated facilities and services? What are the personal and professional competencies, responsibilities, accountabilities, and commitments to the Mayo Clinic of all of its institutional members?

Because of the venerated positions of medical and academic institutions in our society, we have excused them from the challenge of the question: "Is organizational change our only hope in meeting the compelling competitive demands—no longer just domestically, but also globally?" If these institutions' leaders do not accept the opportunity and take the responsibility to educate their constituents, can they realistically expect professional employees to change and to own the problem? Will the members of these institutions continue to accept the government's intrusion and dictation of the answer? Or will they continue selfishly to deny their own organization, forgetting that Alexander Woollcott once observed, "None but a mule denies his own."

The current State of Oregon Medical Services Plan exemplifies an innovative way of dealing with this dilemma. The plan is an aggressive public initiative to determine, define, and articulate the right health care system for the State of Oregon and the competitive criteria for doing that job right. There is to be no compromise in the quality of product or service. There is to be a clear definition of the common good of the state's constituents. The plan identifies the reasons for change and requires citizens to become literate about the facts, to understand the data, to comprehend the consequences, and then to commit themselves to the plan. This change requires the identification of the needs and expectations of Oregon's citizens, the necessary financial resources, the necessary capital investment in facilities and technology, and the competence and commitment of health care employees. It must rationally address personal, professional, and organizational perspectives as the entire system moves toward the common good. This plan conspicuously applies the principles of the Frost-Scanlon process as it comprehensively includes every member of the constituency of patients and employees. The plan candidly and coura-geously presents the realities of society's limited ability to pay and the need for justice and fairness for every citizen. The development of this initiative is currently interrupted by recent federal legislation defining the availabil-ity of healthcare-related services.

Any time you make a sweeping change like this that affects a lot of different oper-ations within the company . . . we have the involvement of all the different areas affected by the change. That is only fair. Production has to see it; quality control has to see it; and of course the customer has to approve it to begin with.
—Gordon, packing designer, Donnelly Corp.

Even though these organizations have trouble answering the question "What is the right job today?" a second question needs to be addressed. "What are the criteria for doing that job right?" With health care costs in the United States exceeding those of industrial nations in the world, with the national failure to serve the minimum health needs, with the bank-ruptcies of hospitals, clinics, and independent practices—with all of this evidence confronting us—it's clear that the health care industry still has not answered either of these questions satisfactorily.

There have been a few sincere attempts by leaders in educational and health care institutions to educate their constituents to the alarming and changed realities. In these institutions the process of knowing, under-standing, and accepting the reasons for change is different, if not more difficult, than in other organizations because of the sophistication and independence of the majority of the employees. There are a few coura-geous leaders: Francis C. Oakley, president of Williams College, Robert Galvin, chairman of Motorola, and Dr. Mitchell T. Rabkin, president of Beth Israel Hospital in Boston. These gentlemen are faithfully telling the story that past performances, practices, and relationships are no longer appropriate or adequate—they are indeed obsolete. Citizens, consumers, patients, clients, and students have been shouting a similar message but have been heard by only a few. The government has introduced its own political solutions. We—the private citizen and our society—are paying the unconscionable costs.

One of the most exciting and promising instances of new accountabil-ity is the revolutionary change at Beth Israel Hospital in Boston. It has

Success Story

**Service With a Smile
From a Familiar Face**

An exciting pilot program that combines the support roles of environmental services, nutrition services, and transportation services is underway on 6 Feldberg. The *support assistant* role was developed to improve continuity of support to patients and their nurses, decrease the number of different people who enter patients' rooms daily, and continue to provide quality patient care.

The new support assistants clean rooms, make beds, provide transportation to and from tests and procedures, transport specimens to the laboratories, and deliver and clear meal trays for 10 to 11 patients on the unit. An important benefit of the program is the opportunity for support assistants to get to know "their" patients, which enables them to better understand each patient's needs, and enhances their patients' confidence in them.

An interdepartmental work team representing administration, environmental services, nursing, nutrition services, and transportation services worked to develop specific tasks and guidelines to incorporate into the new role. In this role, the support assistants have the opportunity to develop more personalized, professional relationships with patients and staff on the unit, which leads to greater job satisfaction, and patients have the sense of security that comes from knowing who they can count on seeing day after day. Team members continually work together to make further improvements to the program.

The program's goals are to improve the quality of services we provide for patients, stabilize or decrease costs, and enrich the working environment of support services employees. All aspects of the program will be evaluated after a six-month period including service quality, cost effectiveness, and patient and employee satisfaction. Based on that evaluation, the team will determine whether this new role will be incorporated on other patient units.

For more details on this successful P R E P A R E / 2 1 effort and the individuals involved, see the September issue of the Examiner.

3

Figure 6. Beth Isreal Hospital of Boston "Success Story"

been traditional in hospitals that nutrition, environmental, housekeeping, and transportation services in the various medical divisions were isolated, fragmented, and occupationally protected. Physicians and nurses were the personnel on whom patients depended for survival and services. Organizational hierarchies and status maintained this state of affairs. Yet at the heart of the organization was a great cadre of people who supplied and maintained cleanliness, orderliness, sanitation, technology and equipment, light bulbs, patient transportation, therapy, and treatments. These people had few academic degrees and sometimes little fluency in English. They did have compassion, willing hands, and friendly voices. Usually a resource of unexplored potential, these employees came and stayed for the right reasons. Under Beth Israel's PREPARE/21 (Prepare for the 21st Century) process, the organization seriously and sincerely reevaluated the performance, practices, and relationships of these people. The hospital focused specifically on "doing the right job" (what would meet patients' needs) and "doing the job right" (how to best accomplish that). The report above (fig. 6) describes the new day for hundreds of competent and committed employees at "BI." It represents a major and professional revolution in having the opportunity *now* to take responsibility and then accepting responsibility *now* for serving the hospital's patients in the best way possible.

Present and ineluctable social, economic, and political demands are compelling the changes at Beth Israel. Professional arrogance and administrative independence have become intolerable in any organization, especially when they become barriers to change. Is it possible to get the attention of and to enlighten already highly educated and trained professionals to become literate, responsible, and accountable as organizational members? Yes, though it is a staggering challenge for leaders and for all of us, whoever we are and wherever we are. The Frost-Scanlon process, with its deliberate and aggressive attitude toward change, is one way to meet this challenge. The Frost-Scanlon process includes professional employees in organizational life, its demands, and its rewards.

Once convinced of the need to become literate, professional members of academic and medical institutions must answer the next question: "Are you able and willing to own the problem?" The answer has an unambiguous impact on their personal professional identities and loyalties. The responses are usually varied. Some people will answer "no." Some highly competent and experienced professionals may decide to become entrepreneurs; others may be in positions to retire; still others will rise to and accept both personally and professionally ownership of the problem.

The third question will be the decisive one: "Is this the organizational team with the requisite competence, gifts, and commitment to win, survive, succeed, and flourish?" The evaluation session including these academic and medical professionals will be so colored by their well-established professional egos that special attention must be focused on the criteria for the team's success. This session may become truly inspirational if the occasion evokes not only legitimate, but essential, revelations of the unique competencies and achievements of these colleagues. The experience may elicit real collegial admiration and appreciation; it can even stimulate the vision, potential, and excitement of expanded organizational collaborations.

As I have already suggested, I highly recommend a confidential straw vote to answer the third question. The more sophisticated the group, the more they discount any protection for their identities (egos). Precisely because their professional identity must not compromise the integrity of the decision, I always urge a secret vote with a strenuous caution to give an honest answer and not an accommodating response. These professionals need more help than they are able and willing to admit in honestly addressing and accepting personal and professional change. Since confessions are good for the soul but hard on the ego, a confidential vote is a procedural favor. *If* the process ever advances this far, then you have arrived at the exciting possibility of developing genuine participation. The Ad Hoc Committee has a genuine opportunity to create an instrument that an organization has not had before, impacting every member personally, professionally, and organizationally. Professionals are generally creative in research, teaching, and the delivery of services. They are familiar with professional excellence in performance and are acquainted with ingenious methodologies. They have had little experience in exploring organizational-relationship potentials. They may not even see the need for a process that includes all members—not least of all, their subordinates—that identifies, facilitates, and assures the organization's survival and success.

I was a tool in other companies. In this company, I'm a family member. I have a say here. The people I work with have something to say. The system pulls them along. The more you participate, the more opportunity you have.
　　　　　　—Jim, plant engineering services, Herman Miller, Inc.

To reach this point in the Frost-Scanlon process requires a rare blend of leadership competence, skills, and commitment. John A. Hannah, president of Michigan State University for twenty-five years, was a conspicuous example. He *enabled* the institution to adapt its prestigious agricultural research, innovative teaching, and penetrating extension service into the post-World War II era of Michigan's industrialization, all the while helping burgeoning numbers of veterans returning from the war to capitalize on promising academic opportunities. After helping to reshape the postwar academic world, he *enabled* the institution to recognize and respond innovatively to worldwide emerging needs, consistent with the land grant philosophy. Faculty members were continually challenged and stretched in their research, teaching, and service opportunities and responsibilities for changing domestic and worldwide needs—agricultural, industrial, economic, social, and political. There was something for every faculty member and every academic discipline, as well as for the supporting administrative employees.

Let me give a few examples. John Hannah convinced six senior faculty members and their families to establish and develop the Escola des Administracao des Empresas at Sao Paulo, Brazil. Each faculty member, including me, took two year appointments from 1950 to 1960. The prestigious Gertulio Vargas Foundation cosponsored this aggressive industrial management graduate school of business administration, the first in South America. What an idea for stretching faculty members and expanding our experience beyond the ordinary! Later, in 1964, I responded to another of Hannah's requests, this time to teach at the exciting and innovative Land Grant University Experiment at the University of Nigeria in Nsukka, instituted to commemorate Nigeria's independence on 1 October 1960. In this case, John Hannah, besides enriching the experience of the faculty at Michigan State, became the key resource in fulfilling president Nnamdi Azekwe's dream. In 1970, Hannah challenged his faculty to participate in the Agricultural Economics—Agricultural/Industrial Development and Marketing Project in Korea. In all of these assignments, the faculty were not placed under any pressure to accept. President Hannah made the opportunity so clear in purpose, priority, and consequences that the commitment, both personal and professional, was easy and gratifying. The families became the heroes.

I have already mentioned Dr. Mitchell T. Rabkin, president of Beth Israel Hospital in Boston, who inaugurated a process in 1986 to educate all of the institution's research, teaching, and health care delivery members to *what day it was* for them personally, professionally, and organizationally. He conveyed to the staff a genuine sense of urgency: "After all, who was worrying about the next century?" Dr. Rabkin enabled them to realize that the Twenty-first century began *Now*. Dr. Rabkin continues to introduce the staff to community, state, and national competitive realities; it has become a permanent part of his job. He stresses the three concerns for improved performances of quality and competency, effective and efficient practices, and exciting collaborative relationships.

Summary of the Ad Hoc Committee

From my experiences with clients in industrial, service, and academic organizations, I would summarize the Ad Hoc Committee's chief goal to be—

> the creation of a rational working environment that recognizes the dignity of each member and challenges the potential of every member in achieving the organization's mandate.

The word *create* implies the infinite diversity of organizational situations and realities. There are no answer books to provide easily available and adaptable programs. The unique givens in each organization require the leader to define them as special organizational opportunities and responsibilities. The word *rational* is the key root word because it focuses and disciplines every element to the logic of its own reality. Only an acceptance of reality gives authenticity, validity, and reliability to the management process. Rational also means that the work environment will not be capriciously governed, that its processes are open to everyone's questions and understanding. *Working environment* is an all-inclusive description not only of employees' immediate working experience, but also of personal and organizational context, both domestic and global. In *recognizing the dignity of each person*, the Ad Hoc Committee—and the Frost-Scanlon process in general—welcomes the inclusion of all human dimensions and affirms the heterogeneous nature of our world. The word *challenge* declares that the organization expects everyone to increase personal and professional effectiveness and efficiencies in meeting the increasingly competitive demands of customers. *Potential* implies that in every employee lie competencies, contributions, and commitments previously unknown, unused, ignored, or unexploited. We would do well to remember Jay Hall's claim in *The Competence Process* and *The Competence Connection*, "Unused competence is quickly interpreted as incompetence." It is a resource waiting to be recognized and challenged. *Achieving the*

79

organization's mandate expresses a corporate direction and an aggregate momentum more demanding and disciplining than anyone's personal or professional ambitions. Ideally, we all see and feel a commitment to corporate objectives as significant and rewarding to each of us.

One of the great things about Scanlon that I appreciate about it, at least as it works at Donnelly, people feel quite free to be critical. You are always explaining, putting things in context. . . . I just think it is real hard work. It pays off if you do it.

—Kay, systems development, Donnelly Corp.

This definition of the Ad Hoc Committee's opportunity and responsibility to create a rational working environment describes its primary objective. This creative objective is well illustrated in *Industry Week's* report (21 January 1991) on Bob Galvin's leadership at Motorola.

But discipline, like charity, begins at home. That's what Motorola discovered a decade ago: Expecting much better products, buyers were leaving Motorola for Japanese competitors that had an unmatched devotion to quality products and services. In response, Motorola set an eyebrow-raising goal in 1981; a tenfold improvement in quality within five years.

Five years later, influenced by further discussions with customers, Mr. Galvin & Co. set an even more ambitious goal—a tenfold improvement in product and service quality by 1989, at least 100-fold improvement by 1991, and Six Sigma by 1992.

Six Sigma is the statistician's way of saying 3.4 defects per million, or 99.99966% perfect. At Motorola, everyone, whether in a corporate office or on a shop floor, is now learning to speak and think in Six Sigma. It's an all-pervasive, continuously improving quality campaign dependent on education and training ($100,000,000 a year), total management commitment, and practice, practice, practice.

In all institutions with a wide range of personal and professional competencies, I do believe the definition of participation is generic: *it is the opportunity that only management can provide and the responsibility that only the members can take to influence the decisions in one's areas of competence— ownership.* In the Frost-Scanlon process, constructive participation can

80

only occur among a literate group. Participation remains the only real way to cope with external change and institute change inside an organization. But for participation to take root and thrive, it must be accompanied by equity, the third principle of the Frost-Scanlon process.

CHAPTER FOUR

THE THIRD PRINCIPLE: EQUITY

Introduction: Equity for the Investors—Customers, Shareholders, and Employees

After establishing the organizationwide processes of reality education and responsible participation and ownership, the third focus and responsibility of the Ad Hoc Committee is to develop the process of accountability, which will implement and fulfill the third principle of the Frost-Scanlon process: equity. In considering the elements of an organization's mandate (customer, physical resources, financial resources, and human resources), external reality imposes imperatives on the organization and its management: the interests of customers, investors, and employees. The primary management complexity in a free enterprise economy is to find an equitable balance among these three interests. In a diagram, an equilateral triangle would represent an ideal balance among them (see fig. 7).

The customer would rightly sit at the apex of that triangle. Without customers, investors and employees would not be needed. Historically, customers' demands have not always come first. Witness the arrogant disregard of customers by the automotive company management, reinforced by egocentric union contracts over several decades. When better options became available, customers enthusiastically bought cars and services from Honda, Toyota, Volkswagon, Audi, and Volvo. These disenchanted customers impacted not only the auto industry, but also the national economy. There is only a vague interest among customers that a particular producer keep its products on the market.

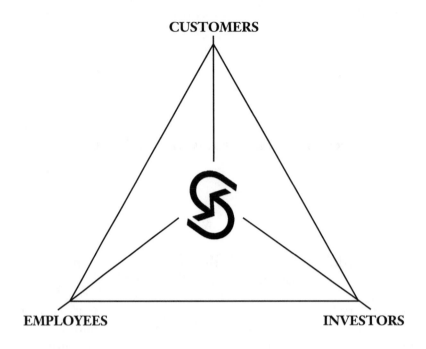

Figure 7. Diagram of Organizational Equity

But, whoever your customers are, if they find that they can buy a Japanese tire that's just as good as yours or better for the same amount of money, then they're going to do it. If you aren't aware of what your competition is or what your customer wants, you're in trouble.

—Bullard, chemical engineer, Firestone Tire

Analogously, patients and students have become increasingly free to search out the most favorable returns on their important investments in superior medical services and academic programs. Personal survival and career opportunities justify a hard look at institutional service providers. Furthermore, car buyers, critically ill patients, and students have little concern for the financial returns to capital investors.

Therefore the establishment and maintenance of balance among the three parties falls to employees and management. The organization must solicit capital investors to furnish facilities, equipment, technology, and supporting infrastructure to enable employees to deliver the required products or services. Still, financial investors can be as demanding, independent, and self-serving as customers. In the past, there seemed to be a personalized loyalty or committed interest in following one's investment over time, especially when it backed a technological breakthrough or a conspicuous entrepreneur. Today, investors' attention spans are short. The criteria for satisfactory financial performance are mechanical and almost system-controlled, exercised by aggregate trusts and pension fund groups. Consequently, the financial market is almost inhumanly competitive; capital investors are relentlessly self-serving. Today, even the fulfillment of sound and prolonged good performance is not enough. Investors seem to expect a surprising and better-than-predicted performance.

We depend on our investors. If we waste their money and don't give them a return on it, they're going to pull their money out. Then we're in trouble.
—Bullard, chemical engineer, Firestone Tire

Twenty years ago, Walter Scott, executive vice president of Motorola and godfather of Motorola's Participative Management Program, took the challenge of the accountability process to Gottlieb Memorial Hospital in Melrose Park. As chairman of the hospital's board of directors representing investors, Scott stunned the entire hospital organization—administration, professional staff, and service members—by announcing the board's decision to freeze the budget for one year. The board was convinced after thorough study that the freeze was necessary to assure investors' equity and the institution's survival. Scott advised the hospital administration that the board would provide assistance from one of three consultant groups to implement the change. The administrators could choose the group.

The administrators and consultant began to identify the right job for Melrose Memorial *now* and the criteria for doing that job right. It was to be an institutional revolution involving every member of the organization. The most convincing development was the establishment of a process of accountability for doing the right job and doing that job right. The epitome of this process was a daily audit by two physicians (an internist and a surgeon) and two staff nurses, all elected by their peers. The predictable daily audit at ten o'clock was the sign of undeniable and unforgiving accountability for changed performance, practices, and relationships. Patients, investors, and hospital personnel were markedly advantaged as the hospital acknowledged the necessity of change—a radical, but rational change—for it to continue to serve the Melrose Park community.

The egocentricity of the interests and demands of both customers and investors places the burden of performance and accountability on the organization's leadership and membership. In the case of Gottlieb Memorial, Walter Scott's dynamic leadership and the hospital staff responded to investors' demand for change. How, under these circumstances, does an organization's leadership establish the equitable right and claims of employees? Sometimes, the use of the words "right" and "claims" is challenged when considering the employees' position and roles. However, if we are to be consistent, then our vocabulary should be consistent. Of what do employees' rights consist? They may not be monetary. A major employee claim must surely be the right to organizational life and citizenship by becoming literate, taking the opportunity management has provided to become responsible, becoming accountable, and developing increasing competence. When customers demanded, in Motorola's terms, products and service at a six-sigma level, they established an equitable right and claim for the fulfillment of that imperative. When financial investors responded to a call for funds under specific risk conditions, they established an equitable right and claim to a certain return. Likewise, when employees accept employment, they establish an equitable right and claim to become organizationally literate, to have the opportunity to take the responsibility of influencing decisions in their area of competence, to be held personally and professionally accountable, and to be enabled to become increasingly competent through education, training, and experience in doing the right job and meeting the criteria for doing that job right.

Just as any infant in the United States has a right to become a literate, responsible, and accountable contributing member of a family and society, any employee has a self-evident right to belong—in a meaningful way—to the organization he or she has joined. The consequences of denying a child the right to contribute to society are well documented by illiteracy rates and the numbers of unskilled and unemployable people. When the equitable rights and claims of employees are disregarded or voided, management jeopardizes the possibility of identifying and engaging the attention, accountability, and commitment of all employees in satisfying the competitive demands of customers and investors. Management disenfranchises them and prevents them from owning the problem or achieving the organization's mandate. Management excludes them from working for their own and the organization's survival. Such a situation is patently unacceptable.

If customers and investors gain their returns at the expense of employees, which is possible although usually short-lived, management is ignoring, discounting, or denying the priorities, relationships, and interdependencies among these three groups. Can there be any question or confusion about the essential nature of education, responsible ownership, and accountability? Are the four principles of the Frost-Scanlon process (identity, participation, equity, and competence) and their respective processes (education, ownership, accountability, and commitment) luxuries? Without fidelity to these fundamental factors and processes, doesn't management significantly endanger the possibility and potential of fulfilling the priority rights and expectations of customers and financial investors? Is there any industry or institution now addressing global competition that has not experienced the consequences of favoring one group at the expense of another? In other words, if employees' *equitable* rights are not established and realized, the organization will simply not be able to satisfy its customers and investors.

The bottom—and I'll hang strong on this—when you begin to look at a triangle, the largest part is the bottom, and as it goes up, it gets smaller and smaller. And the employees are your masses. That's where your largest group is, your employees. It is those people that's got to make the change.
                                        —Wallace, warehouse employee, Firestone Tire

---

Mr. D. J. DePree, the founder of Herman Miller, stated the concept succinctly forty years ago: "A business is rightly judged by its products and services—but it must also face scrutiny and judgment as to its humanity." These words are carved in the cornerstone of the main manufacturing facility of Herman Miller, Inc.

The Accountability Process: The Customer

If an organization truly believes in the primary position of customers (patients, students, clients), it is essential that the Ad Hoc Committee develop a valid, reliable, and rapid feedback system from them, one that works to the mutual advantage of customers *and* employees. Equally important, the feedback must be transmitted through an effective and expeditious communication system. Only customers can verify that the organization or institution is doing the right job. Customers' responses measure employees' ability (competencies) and willingness (commitment) to do the job right. We have returned to the first essential steps of education—knowing, understanding, and comprehending. Employees should never be left to question or speculate on the consequences of their performances, personally and professionally. Is the dissatisfied customer able and willing to wait for remedial action or improved response? Only when customers' attitudes are known does an employee have the opportunity to accept responsibility for satisfying their increasing demands for better quality and services. Responsiveness is a legitimate return expected by customers; their feedback is a legitimate return expected by employees.

The way that we do that is we have our goals and through the equity plan, the way it's set up, is we have targets that we set up and we feel that they are do-able, they're realistic. If we make our goals, customers will be getting service, the investors will be getting a good return on their dollar, and we will be rewarded through our bonus system for doing that. If we don't provide a good investment return for the investor, then we don't get any bonus either. If we don't provide good quality and timely products for our customers, then we don't get our bonus. It's all tied together. We share in the good times, and we share in the bad times.
—Pat, production coordinator, Herman Miller, Inc.

This process of accountability must be a regular and conspicuous companywide audit report in which every employee has a vested interest. The process genuinely actualizes the opportunity employees should have daily to "know what day it is," enabling them to know something today that they did not know yesterday—a change. Now they have the opportunity—and hopefully will take the responsibility—to do something about it before it is too late.

This early Herman Miller monthly accountability report (see fig. 8) illustrates specific criteria for satisfying customers' expectations for complete, correct, and on-time shipments. An interesting company financial criterion involving accounts receivable (the number of days the accounts are outstanding) is quite directly related to customers' satisfaction. Customers completely satisfied with product installation and shipment pay their bills more quickly than customers who find their installations unsatisfactory for any reason. Consequently, all Herman Miller employees are really advantaged by satisfying their customers with superior products and service performances. Employees have sustained employment, and continued opportunities to learn, to contribute, to raise their competence, and to increase their earnings and bonuses. The bonus is tied directly to customer-provided ratings of product quality and service. Bonuses rise only upon genuine improvements and change in product quality and service—change and improvement is the name of the game.

Performance to Plan Score

Customer Service	O/I	H/S	IS	Operations	Corporate	Average	Total
On-time Shipments							
Correct Shipments							
Past Dues							
Rapid Response Index							
Effective Use of Labor	O/I	H/S	IS	Operations	Corporate	Average	Total
Orders							
Production							
Projects							
Administrative Service							
Effective Use of Material	O/I	H/S	IS	Operations	Corporate	Average	Total
Inventory Investment							
Scrap							
Shrinkage							
Effective Use of Money	O/I	H/S	IS	Operations	Corporate	Average	Total
Expense Control							
Net Revenue							
Accounts Receivable							
Material Price Variance							

Performance Score

Points

Figure 8. Herman Miller, Inc. Performance to Plan Chart

This format has continually changed in response to more aggressive customer demands for superior quality and efficient services. The current monthly report is a customerwide data base created from intensive audits of customer satisfaction. The "quality audits," as the company terms them, are performed by appropriate professional members and company officers, geared to the complexity and volume of the installation. This process of accountability has been well received by customers and has become an efficient and convincing way of educating employees and management. The full potential of these communications from customers has yet to be realized.

The Accountability Process: The Shareholder

This illustration (see fig. 9) is an early attempt to become more accountable to capital investors or owners.

The increasing demand from shareholders to improve their equity in the company and their return prompted more specific criteria of accountability in the current monthly reports. This accountability for the optimal

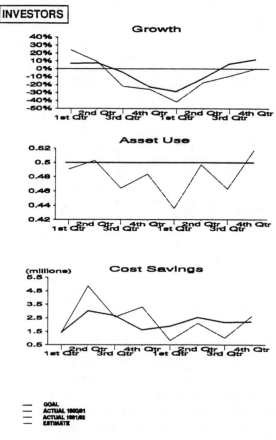

Figure 9. Herman Miller, Inc. Investor Criteria

operation of facilities and equipment suggests various measurements such as the sales per square foot of a sales outlet; the efficient scheduling of hospital operating rooms, university laboratories, and teaching facilities; the scheduled hours of operating MRI (Magnetic Resonance Imaging), CAT scanners, Herman Miller's costly Torwegge machines, or Donnelly Corporation's "clean rooms." Several companies are committed to their facilities functioning as "people places"—(for example, the admission areas of hospitals and the break areas of manufacturing plants). It is important that this company commitment to a better return on assets not be considered merely a public relations effort. Employees should be committed to a substantially greater return on the investment in their people places than in less humane work sites. In general, all employees must be aware of the demands of investors, just as they must be aware of the demands of customers. This awareness is part of being a literate employee in the 1990s.

The 1985 Herman Miller Annual Report introduces all of the company's employees. Their remarks, scattered through the report, express their feelings about ownership and accountability (see fig.10).

The Accountability Process: The Human Resources

Another area of monthly accountability on the report is the effective use of labor. Orders/Lead Time is a report of the Sales and Marketing members' ability to provide adequate lead times on their entered orders in order to facilitate the most efficient scheduling of production. Productivity directly measures manufacturing employees' productivity efficiency. Projects/Critical Services is a report of the performances of the research, design, and development members in performing their assignments on time and within their prescribed budgets. This section provides a perspective on the range of activities as well as the professional competencies required to perform them. It is a measure of the performance of the entire team.

. . . because when a problem occurs, then they will know exactly whom to come back to. There is no way you can point a finger at another person. I am the one accountable for it. I'm the one who did it. I'm the one who is responsible for whatever consequence. I've learned to accept that.

—Michael, production employee, Firestone Tire

91

Herman Miller, Inc.   **1985 Annual Report**   **SAY HELLO TO THE OWNERS!**

Figure 10. Herman Miller, Inc. Annual Report

Accountability is more specifically documented by the monthly report of employees' suggestions for improving the quality of products, services, and efficiency, and for reducing costs. The Donnelly Corporation reports illustrate this monthly process of accountability and document their increasing success between 1986 and 1992 (see fig.11).

IDEA$ (Fiscal Year 1991/ 92)

Dollars Saved

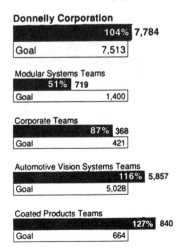

Donnelly Corporation

111%	$9,784,830
Goal	$8,782,500

Modular Systems Teams

116%	$4,167,654
Goal	$3,600,000

Corporate Teams

89%	$624,804
Goal	$700,000

Automotive Vision Systems Teams

96%	$2,900,191
Goal	$3,027,500

Coated Products Teams

144%	
Goal	$1,455,000	$2,092,181

Number of Suggestions

Donnelly Corporation

104%	7,784
Goal	7,513

Modular Systems Teams

51%	719
Goal	1,400

Corporate Teams

87%	368
Goal	421

Automotive Vision Systems Teams

116%	5,857
Goal	5,028

Coated Products Teams

127%	840
Goal	664

Figure 11. Donnelly Corporation IDEA$ Suggestion Program

One of the most exciting and promising developments of accountability is the revolutionary change at Beth Israel Hospital in Boston that we have already discussed. Under its PREPARE/21 (PREPARE for the 21st Century) process, the organization seriously and sincerely reevaluated all of its various services in light of the *patients'* needs. The evaluation extended beyond the obvious roles of doctors and nurses to the contributions of dietary, maintenance, housekeeping, transport, laboratory, laundry, utilities, and translator services. The result was an eager acceptance of more personal involvement and volunteered responsibility for becoming accountable as an integrated organization serving its patients.

Herman Miller supplements its monthly reports by an annual accountability through the Idea Club. Membership in the Idea Club is earned either by the number of quality suggestions or by the dollar amount of savings actually gained from the implementation of a suggestion. The following excerpt from their regular employee publication, *Connections*, illustrates the widely experienced spirit and celebration of accountability (see fig. 12). (I use the word celebration, because I believe the process of personal and professional accountability is the essential element in identifying and achieving positive self-worth.) Even personally confronting less-than-adequate performance is a necessary and promising process of documenting self-worth. If my performance is not important enough to make a difference and to be held accountable, then my self-worth does not rise above zero.

⊔ herman miller   Idea Club Edition   Mid-August 1992

CONNECTIONS

Idea Club Sixty-nine individuals, three teams inducted this year

Sixty-nine employees and three teams were inducted into the 1992 Idea Club on July 16 in Grandville.

They contributed a significant proportion of the company's 1,449 accepted and 1,222 implemented suggestions for the March 1991-through-February 1992 Idea Club year. And they contributed more than their share of the $6,553,080 of suggestion-generated savings for the fiscal year 1991-92.

Figure 12. Herman Miller, Inc. Employee Newsletter—Idea Club

The process of accountability is third in the development sequence. It follows literacy (as required by identity) and taking responsibility for owning the problem (as required by participation), thereby making a difference. It should be apparent that if you don't expect much, you are seldom disappointed. The process of accountability establishes the legitimacy and potential of the employee. It legitimizes high expectations, validates the organization's drive to improve, and documents the importance of the chief executive officer's mandate.

So we then take that information and take it to the organization. Here's our performance. Each officer has to get up and talk about results to goal. We are hooked up nationally and open to challenge about why we didn't perform and what we need to do. Then the challenge goes back to the organization. The next step is each one of those people in those meetings should go back to their work teams and say, "Here's where we're performing well; here's where the challenge is. Let's come up with solutions to meet those challenges." You can't get more integrated and penetrating than that.

—Michele, vice president for people, Herman Miller, Inc.

The Ad Hoc Committee Assignment

The Ad Hoc Committee's job of developing a proposal to turn the Frost-Scanlon process into an operational program is a comprehensive responsibility. The discussion thus far implies three features and suggests three committees: the Education Committee, the Participation Committee, and the Equity Committee.

The Ad Hoc Committee's assignment develops a specific process of accountability to assure the rights and claims of customers, capital investors, and employees. The meeting of criteria for accountability depends on employees becoming literate and responsive to the demands and expectations of each group of investors—including customers. Therefore, the criteria are not arbitrary but must clearly represent the external imperatives. Valid and reliable data sources must be established from investors and related directly to employees for understanding and response. These data should be directed toward satisfying customers with superior quality of products and services, building investors' confidence in equity improvement and dividends, and convincing employees that this organization provides the best employment opportunity.

If you're going to be accountable for something, then you have to have some voice in determining what it is. . . . And, if indeed, you have participated in the goal setting, then I think it's absolutely fair and it's responsible that one should be held accountable that those things happen. And no one is naive enough to believe that, just because you put a plan down on paper, even though there is a lot of thought given to it, that it's therefore going to happen.

—Dick, president, Herman Miller, Inc.

The company is most advantaged by assigning its most competent and innovative financial officer to direct the development of this process of accountability. In every organization in which I have served as a consultant, financial officers have genuine and persistent misgivings as to the need for and appropriateness of the Frost-Scanlon process. They predict limited cost savings and little effect on the bottom line. They anticipate little change in their department and its function. These feelings were best expressed by Lynn Broadfoot, a senior and widely respected controller at Firestone Tire. The following is from Mr. Broadfoot's presentation to several companies exploring the possibilities of the Frost-Scanlon process.

A Corporate Controller's Point of View

1. The workers won't buy it. They prefer conventional piecework plans.
2. The Executive Committee of the board of directors won't buy it. Besides, I don't relish the traumatic idea of appearing before them to try and sell it!
3. The plan requires distribution of too much confidential information to factory personnel.
4. Factory personnel do not understand accounting. A major educational program would therefore be required.
5. The plan seems to be designed primarily for those companies that are in a "back to the wall" situation with shutdown a likely alternative. We do not fit that category.

6. The time is not right for us since we are new. Let's wait four or five years until we have matured under our present system. (By then I'll be retired and won't have all those problems to wrestle with!)
7. The whole thing seems like a somewhat socialistic scheme to give away our profits.
8. I can't wait to meet that professor and get the opportunity to give him my thoughts.

The leadership and education process of John Boettner secured Broadfoot's commitment to change, even over objections like the above. Broadfoot demonstrated his personal and professional ownership by chairing the Ad Hoc Committee on Equity and Accountability and developing a credible and effective accountability data system. In educating Firestone's 1,900 employees, the conspicuous personal and professional integrity, competence, and commitment of Boettner, the general manager, and Broadfoot, the born-again comptroller, resulted in a 98 percent margin of approval in the straw vote. The system enabled every employee to change, not least of all the bright MBAs on Broadfoot's staff, who competed for the opportunity to manage production departments, where they could make a more conspicuous difference.

In every organization, therefore, the financial officer should develop and introduce with the Ad Hoc Committee the process of accountability. This fiscal officer's personal and professional identity, integrity, and competence must be conspicuously functional. Under this special leadership, the assignment of the Ad Hoc Committee on Equity begins with the unique education about what the organization *has been* accountable for and its record to date. Then the committee focuses on the criteria for competitive *performance*, the critical evaluation of current professional and institutional *practices*, and the potential for more effective personal and more efficient professional *relationships*. The gist of the principle of equity is "To whom, for whom, and with whom are the employees and the institution accountable?" The spirit and essence of change—what has been is no longer good enough—should prevail.

During the work of the Ad Hoc Committee, a pleasant surprise seems to occur in almost every situation. The Ad Hoc Committee members, including somewhat entrenched union contract bargainers, usually suggest that employee accountability be even more rigorous than management might expect. A frequent comment is "I never knew. . . ." The experience provides education in a believable setting.

97

Of course, there should be a determined effort to develop a definition of accountability that serves all employees. However, the Ad Hoc Committee's report should certainly allow the chief executive officer confidently to hold every employee personally and professionally accountable for fulfilling the expectations of customers, investors, and employees. The process and instrument should enable the chief executive officer to ask the right questions, to challenge the right members, to engage the right resources and competencies, and to tell the whole story. The document should help the chief executive officer become vulnerable in serving the organization and welcoming the questions, "What happened?" "How come?" and "What is going to be done about it?" The leader is uniquely advantaged by hearing the most legitimately embarrassing questions about inadequate performance, inefficient practices, and compromised relationships.

At this point in summarizing the Ad Hoc Committee's development of a proposal for the organization, I believe it would be genuinely helpful to review the experiences of Motorola employees. You will notice immediately that the Frost-Scanlon process at Motorola is not a program. It is a process of management. You will see that the development of the Frost-Scanlon process demands unique creativity from every organization. And you will see that this process can bring the best in an organization to the surface.

The following article, by James O'Toole (in *New Management*, 3:2, Fall 1985), describes the experience of participation at Motorola and the critical place of the steering committee.

The Motorola PMP

Throughout the 1970s, the engine of change at Motorola was what they called their Participative Management Program (PMP). It is misnamed, for it is not a program at all; rather, it has become synonymous with the way they manage at Motorola. Building on the highly participative style of founder Paul Galvin, Motorola's managers have created a system in which employees now have a greater stake in Motorola than Japanese workers have in the best-run corporations in Japan. As one Motorola employee explained to me, underscoring the differences between conditions at Motorola and those in Japanese companies, "Like the Japanese, we play softball and volleyball on the excellent facilities the corporation provides for us. But, unlike the Japanese, we play when we want to, not on cue!"

The Motorola system of worker participation is much simpler to describe than it was to create, for it was not easy to devise a system in which employees could all legitimately feel they have a say in management. To begin, Motorola recognized that it would be impossible for all of its 60,000 domestic employees to function effectively if they each acted in isolation. For purposes of coordination, then, Motorola employees have been grouped into teams of some 50 to 250 workers. Each employee shares in a common bonus pool with his or her other team members. The idea is that the people in each pool will be responsible for their own performance, as measured by production costs and materials controlled by the team, by quality, by production levels, by inventory of stock and finished goods, by housekeeping standards, and by safety records. Whenever an idea proposed by a team leads to a cost reduction, or to production that exceeds a target, all team members share in the gains through bonuses (the average varies between 8% and 12%).

This system resembles the Scanlon process that has been successful for three decades at Herman Miller (see Vol. 1. No. 4 of NM). The genius of the Motorola system is that it has been made to work in a very large corporation. A key element in the successful translation of what was originally a small company idea into big company practice is Motorola's intricate process of communications. Each working team has one of its members on a steering committee at the next higher level in the company (which, in turn, has a member on another committee at the subsequent higher level). The steering committee performs several critical functions:

1. Coordination. A steering committee acts on ideas from a working group that require cooperation with one or more other working groups.
2. Lateral Communication. A steering committee disseminates the ideas or practices of one working group to other groups, thus facilitating organizational learning.
3. Downward Communication. A steering committee insures that each work group has all the managerial information it requires to do its job.
4. Upward Communication. Since each steering committee is linked to the next level steering committee (which, in turn, reports to top management), shop floor issues reach Motorola executives after going through only four levels in the hierarchical chain (This is an extremely flat organizational structure for a company with 95,000 workers worldwide).

5. Control. A steering committee negotiates output standards and measures of performance with the work teams that report to it, a continuing process that builds trust by clearly establishing performance criteria for work teams in advance of the evaluation process.
6. Evaluation. Based on the negotiated measures of performance, a steering committee evaluates the record of the work teams that report to it and allocates the rewards based on a prenegotiated formula.

I think a lot about accountability. Accountability that I have to the person I report to and to my work team members to get the job done, whatever that job is. Accountability to the work team so that they have the resources, they know what's expected, and why, and all that background behind it of the job to be accomplished and how they impact those strategies and goals. How they fit in. I think that there's an accountability that everyone has to the customer. . . . I think of the accountability that we have to investors, and we talk about employee-owners at Herman Miller because most employees are stockholders at Herman Miller.
—*Wayne, corporate business systems, Herman Miller, Inc.*

The Ad Hoc Committee Presents Its Proposal

The completion of the Ad Hoc Committee's proposal is a specific demonstration of the leader having provided employees, motivated by an informed commitment to the organization, with the opportunity to develop and demonstrate a new competence. The Ad Hoc Committee's presentation of its proposal is genuine evidence of its members having accepted a personal and organizational responsibility and their endorsement and advocacy of changes that will affect the performance, practices, and relationships of every employee. The teaching of the key company people appointed to the Ad Hoc Committee by management (sales, financial, and human resource executives) and the learning by every member of the committee are classic examples of a true process of education. The solid and enthusiastic consensus of the Ad Hoc Committee members is a wish that every employee had this unique opportunity to learn, to be responsible, and to be held accountable—all because they were and are involved in a personal and organizational change process. They readily admit the assignment has been personally difficult, requiring study, energy, and time. Satisfaction with the result makes it all worthwhile. The energy impounded in the report must not be left with the chief executive officer, the first to see it. The role of the committee members must shift from creators of a proposal to qualified advocates, speaking first to the chief executive officer and then, if endorsed by the CEO and board of directors, to the entire organization. The following letter captures some of the excitement of an Ad Hoc Committee's work, but more important, it conveys their advocacy of learning, comprehending, and accepting a recommendation to change.

Fellow Employees:

. . . elections took place in which all of us voted for fellow employees to represent us on the *Wilson Plant Employee Participation Plan Ad Hoc Committee*. The Ad Hoc Committee members were charged with the responsibility of formulating all the basics that make up our Employee Participation Plan. A total of 75 representatives were elected and then divided into the three primary subcommittees listed below.

Educational Committee: This group's purpose was to research and determine the need for Wilson to incorporate the Plan. Also, this group was responsible for publishing regular newsletters reporting progress of the Ad Hoc Committee. The assembly and distribution of the attached Employee Participation Plan proposal represents their final task.

Rules and Regulations Committee: This group was faced with the difficult task of developing the guidelines under which the Plan would function. Through many hours of work the committee established the organizational structure of the Plan including the Suggestions System, Production Committees, Screening Committee, and Plan Coordinator. The committee met its objective of establishing rules and regulations that were fair, not burdensome, and which provided for participation in the Plan by everyone.

Formula Committee: This group dealt with the real nuts and bolts of the Plan. They too spent many hours arriving at the final bonus formula. The primary objective here was to provide an equity system that would generate a monthly bonus as a result of our ability to operate the plant more profitably. Items affecting the plant's operation which it was felt were not controllable by us were excluded from the formula.

Following in this proposal book are the results of the efforts of your representatives to formulate an Employee Participation Plan that will allow each of us to play a part in the improved profitability of our plant and our company while receiving an equitable share of that improvement and at the same time making our employment future more secure.

The next step in our future is up to you. For the Plan to be successful it will take the aggressive participation of everyone. In the upcoming acceptance vote, our Plan's future will depend upon a "yes" vote from at least 90% of Firestone and Allied personnel.

Our plan, as presently structured, is good, but probably not perfect. However, the mechanics of the Plan allow for refinement of those areas which do not effectively and fairly serve the interests of the Plan participants or the Company.

As your representatives, we have worked for a plan that will work. We feel we have achieved this objective and strongly recommend that each of you vote "yes" so that the benefits of the Plan may begin to compensate us for the efforts we are both willing and able to put forth. It's up to you!

THE WILSON PLANT EMPLOYEE PARTICIPATION PLAN
AD HOC COMMITTEE

The Ad Hoc Committee document is only a proposal for the sincere consideration of the chief executive officer. He or she accepts the proposal as a working-paper. The chief executive officer evaluates the proposed processes, asking whether it is the most effective and efficient way to fulfill "in the office" the mandated imperatives of the organization. Only the CEO knows what his superiors hold him accountable for. The decision to accept the Ad Hoc Committee proposal, therefore, is exclusively the chief executive officer's opportunity and responsibility. The proposal should become the ultimate instrument for corporate team leadership and followers by establishing the four principles of the Frost-Scanlon process and implementing them. The leader must comprehend that under these circumstances, the leadership role is not cheerleading. Cheerleaders never score a point. The only way to win is to fulfill a competently developed and efficiently executed game plan.

Board of Directors' Endorsement

Inasmuch as the chief executive officer has a significant and conspicuous responsibility to his superiors, as well as to his followers, it is essential, particularly to protect the employees, that the Ad Hoc Committee proposal be studied and sincerely endorsed by the organization's board of

102

directors. Their approval ought not to be pro forma. It should be given only after they study the proposal and challenge the Ad Hoc Committee members as to their confidence in and commitment to their recommendations. Only then should the board of directors take official executive action. The following statement is an example of one such official action. The statement reiterates the mandated imperatives of customers, investors, and employees.

TO: Mr. J. J. Boettner
Wilson Plant
FROM: F. A. Le Page

. . . we were pleased to receive the proposal of the Ad Hoc Committee to install an Employee Participation Plan in Wilson, North Carolina. We appreciate the thorough study and the time commitment required of you in preparing this proposal.

We want to report that the Executive Committee has approved enthusiastically your proposal. We recommend that you proceed to prepare the Wilson employees for their responsibility in evaluating and voting adoption of the Employee Participation Plan.

We would remind you that the adoption of the Plan brings genuine responsibilities:

1. The quality of our product and the satisfaction of our customers must not be sacrificed to quantity of production.
2. The investments of facility, equipment and technology in Wilson must bring a better return in profits.
3. The introduction of an Employee Participation Plan in Wilson will be another Firestone innovation that must succeed as a learning model for other plants.

Based upon your record of the first three years of operation and your careful participation in your proposal, we are confident that the employees at Firestone Wilson will vote responsibly in their own best interests for Firestone Corporation and their families. We will be following your progress with great interest.

F. A. Le Page
Executive Vice President
of the Firestone Tire & Rubber Company

103

The assignment and fulfillment of the Ad Hoc Committee's proposal is a basic application of the first three principles and processes of Frost-Scanlon. The committee members, elected and appointed representatives of employees, confirm that past performances, practices, and relationships are no longer appropriate in serving customers. They recognize the opportunity and accept responsibility for creating and exercising a new process to allow every employee to own service to the customer. Inasmuch as competitive realities are external imperatives, the committee proposes a reliable data system of accountability to produce criteria for fair and balanced equity among customers, investors, and employees.

Management's charge to the Ad Hoc Committee is a conspicuous example of providing to employees the opportunity to create a rational organizational environment in which each employee's dignity is recognized and every employee's potential is challenged. It is essential to remember that the proposal is a recommendation to be accepted, rejected, or altered by management. It is also important to remember that management must recognize the proposal as the committee's mutual personal and professional accountability in visualizing and actualizing companywide commitment to succeed competitively. To have progressed as far as the Ad Hoc Committee's proposal is a genuine achievement and the first step toward real change for the organization.

CHAPTER FIVE

THE FOURTH PRINCIPLE: COMPETENCE

Following in logical sequence, the fourth principle is competence, both a personal quality and qualification. Becoming competent is primarily a personal responsibility. We acquire competence in one area or another to achieve something we desire. The degree of need or the attractiveness of the desired objective influences the effort and priority of acquiring the specific competencies required to achieve a certain goal. Unless we see a need for or desire a certain result, we will not become competent in a skill required to obtain that result. From infancy, competence requires initiative and effort to accomplish some performance or skill. The effort and persistence of an infant learning to walk illustrates a willingness to experience many punishing failures to gain independent mobility. For a child, competent mobility is the key to a world of interesting opportunities, an essential skill needed to explore and capitalize on the perceived world and to pursue the unknown world beyond.

Applying this early life experience of learning to walk to organizational experience, we can see the importance of knowing, understanding, and comprehending the compelling and attractive qualities of reality in stimulating initiative and effort to develop a competent response to that reality. If a child can see no reason to walk, he will not learn. We recognize that, historically, employees have entered and endured their employment world as described and imposed by management. There has been little allowance for, or encouragement of, the freedom to explore and discover—to "walk the talk." Most employees have accepted the limiting myopia of their work space. As Douglas McGregor has pointed out, employees' behavior is directly responsive to this treatment. The current high level of intellectual and skill illiteracy in American organizations should not be surprising. It is not an accident. The resulting lack of responsible, accountable, and committed competencies represent staggering economic and societal problems.

I think that anyone here can be competent, not everyone is naturally that way, but I think that Donnelly provides opportunities to learn how to change. Sometimes it just happens by force. . . . I really feel that I fell into some real neat opportunities to be able to develop a lot of skills, even though I work in production. For me, it wouldn't be worth it to work here without it.

—Bonny, production employee, Donnelly Corp.

Twenty-five years ago, Motorola employees shared with me their gratitude for the personal advantages of their employment—generous fringe benefits, multiple maternity leaves, and so forth. Today, these same employees speak of the *corporate* advantages of their jobs—interesting and challenging classes, manual skills, computer skills, team training, and exposure to the most advanced technology. They are especially aware of the meaning of Motorola's Baldrige Award and the effort required to win it. Their attitude and observations show the partnership commitment of employees and the corporation. They are obviously aware of the personal and professional competencies required to identify, develop, produce, and deliver the right job in the right way.

I suggest again, if it is not too late, that education is the most promising investment, from the cradle to the grave, for every individual, if we are to acquire the competencies essential to survival in a predictably competitive world. In a widely publicized statement, Motorola commits $100,000,000 annually to corporatewide education. The company's overt objective is to enable every employee to become competently accountable for change and the results in the effort to achieve corporate objectives.

If you commit yourself to learn your job to the very best you can, if you give the extra effort, you become more competent on your job. You will learn more about that job. You have to initiate it. Nobody can make you become more competent in your job.

—Jerry, classification and final inspection, Firestone Tire

With the acceptance of the Ad Hoc Committee's report, the role of the organization's leader now becomes that of teacher and educator. Even though the titled opportunity has already been conferred, the identity of the incumbent and the identity of the office are different learning experiences and models of competence for the incumbent and for the rest of the organization. Let me illustrate the differences. When a person is chosen president of an organization that I am serving as a consultant, I am accustomed to write a letter in which I congratulate him or her on the opportunity to *become* president. Even though the title has already been conferred, the person only begins the process of determining, defining, and fulfilling the responsibilities of the office by developing and demonstrating the required competencies at that particular time. This is an opportunity to change that should not be overlooked. The relationship between leader-as-teacher and employee-learners is a novel opportunity for the organization to become something changed: a competitive, responsible, accountable, competent, and committed team.

Some elected or appointed leaders only fulfill the requirements of the office over time and only gradually earn recognition as a servant leader. A new leader needs to grow not only on the job, as he becomes increasingly competent in knowing, understanding, and fulfilling his responsibilities to employees. He also needs to grow *in* the job, as he becomes increasingly competent in knowing, understanding, comprehending, and fulfilling his responsibilities on behalf of employees to their industry, community, nation, and the world. The office provides a set of required qualifications best represented by skills in the organization's management of four areas: customer/marketplace; physical resources; financial resources; and human resources. In my experience, the president's performance in leading the management of these four areas tests his competence in educating employees about the compelling need to change, to become responsible owners, to be accountable, to become competent, and to be committed to achieving the organization's mandate. Lacking a way to succeed personally, who would sincerely commit himself to an organization? And lacking genuine and conspicuous commitment from its leader, what organization can expect employees to become competent enough to succeed competitively?

I think the reward is in the opportunity to grow. . . . The reward comes not only monetarily, but I am given more responsibility.
—Dave, manufacturing manager, Donnelly Corp.

Too often the new president and the organization behave as though he has arrived at the end, rather than at the beginning, of a career. To be perceived by employees as their best means available is a critical, personal, and professional achievement that must be earned by the new leader. Realistically, the president may experience a few professional pratfalls in his new career, being perhaps for the first time publicly exposed in both failure and success. Hopefully, there will be watchful and competent "family-company" support and encouragement. The distinction between occupying an office and becoming a true leader suggests responsibility to become increasingly competent on behalf of the entire organization. It's an understatement to say that employees have a vested interest in competence at the top of their organization.

The president's position as the organization's most competent teacher should become apparent. The message of his unique organizational vision and perspectives should be characteristic and expected of the office. Two examples are Motorola's "going for perfection unto six sigma of quality performance" and Dr. Mitchell Rabkin's challenge to Beth Israel Hospital to PREPARE for the 21st Century. The leader should be conspicuous in orchestrating all of the relevant and urgent literacy, ownership, accountability, and commitment. The president has the singular opportunity and responsibility to vouch publicly for the integrity, authenticity, validity, and reliability of his own and employees' performances, practices, and relationships.

In the role of educator, the president should anticipate and welcome appropriate feedback from inquisitive and involved employees. Employees usually know whether it is appropriate to respond or to ask questions. If the leader's body language and message only preach the company story, employees will politely go away or go to sleep. Remember, as Jay Hall reminds us, "unused competence is quickly interpreted as incompetence." Are employees ready to listen and hear and then respond? Or do they need the company wake-up call? Employees are experientially adept and organizationally competent in assessing whether this occasion is a chance to know, to learn, to challenge, and to ask "How come?" "Why not?" "What happened?" "Who is going to do something about it?" You would sincerely hope that one or two brave souls will run the risk of asking about or even reporting surprising and negative findings or happenings.

Commitment—it is much harder to do. I think that is why it is not practiced. It is like anything else. I think it is like anyone who is really good at anything—a musician, athlete, or a manager, whoever. These people are really good because they have been committed to being good for a really long time. They have been disciplined, and they have worked very hard at it.
—Dwane, chief executive officer, Donnelly Corp.

Without some feedback the leader will not know if the employees have learned anything or if they have understood, comprehended, or accepted the corporate message as relevant, believable, or convincing. Silence is difficult to evaluate objectively. After clearly presenting, at least according to the leader's feelings, the organizational facts of life, a leader's challenge is to develop and ask questions that assess genuine learning. Test questions are professionally difficult to construct. In the evaluation of both teaching and learning, the questions should be part of the Quiz You Cannot Fail that I mentioned in an earlier chapter. For example, Mitchell Rabkin and David Dolins ask at the end of their institution's story the personal and professional question: "What will keep you at Beth Israel Hospital the next ten years?" Don't expect an immediate answer to a meaningful question. Does the leader have the courage and the staying power to wait for the real answers? Out-waiting informed silence is an awesome experience. It is a rare challenge to the leader's competence and integrity.

As in participation and ownership, a question represents an opportunity as well as a possible responsibility. The merit of the question determines the quality of the opportunity provided by the leader. Answering questions is a responsibility for employees to accept or reject. Both actions are conspicuous checks of competence—for both the leader and followers. Do the answers establish and confirm a competent and committed relationship?

This teacher/leader model represents a competency and a personal and professional commitment to competence that one would want every manager or supervisor to demonstrate. The professional teacher prepares daily lesson plans for the students to know the changing contents and dynamics of that day's new assignment and its consequences. Likewise, employees deserve the credible opportunity to know the new day's assignment for better performance, improved practices, and effective relationships before they can wisely accept the responsibility for improvement. From the start of the working day, employees must be assured that at the conclusion there will be personal and professional accountability. Responsibility without expected, timely, and meaningful accountability is a fraudulent relationship between leader and employees. Improved performance tomorrow depends on the confirmation of my worth today and the expectation that tomorrow will raise the ante on my competence. Again, Jay Hall would state that unknown and unchallenged competence is not only a disservice to the organization, it is also a personal and professional tragedy.

Commitment: The Process of Actualizing Competence

The process of commitment is the special opportunity for, and responsibility of, the leader to address for himself and with employees participative ownership, accountability, and competence. President John Kennedy's famous inaugural address described such mutual commitment: "Do not ask what your country can do for you. Ask what you can do for your country." Let me repeat Mitchell Rabkin's and David Dolin's timely challenge to Beth Israel Hospital employees: "What will keep you [committed] at Beth Israel Hospital for the next ten years?" It is the leader's challenge to state the vision and the consequences that provide believable, convincing, and even compelling reasons for placing organizational commitment before personal goals.

The challenge captures personal and professional commitment to change, to become increasingly competent in knowing, owning, and being accountable for the organization's survival and success. The rewards must be assured and demonstrated.

Commitment, however, like competence, is a personal consideration. It is the infant's response to his own evaluation of positive and negative consequences. The decision to commit oneself to increased competence represents a profound and personal change. Employees must decide to accept the given competitive realities—the givens—and either manage the consequences or not. Personal autonomy plays a large part in this decision. Situational and authoritarian coercion can influence the decision, often limiting or preventing commitment. For management to expect an employee's commitment to change and improve without the opportunity to become appropriately competent is grossly unfair. Any attempt to fulfill commitments without the required competence will only result in personal and organizational costs and penalties. The inseparable nature of required competence and organizational commitment must be honestly and candidly evaluated and discussed.

That's how I look at commitment—it's taking the ownership and making it your problem. Not the company's problem, not the customer's problem, it's your problem—opportunity!

—Pat, production coordinator, Herman Miller, Inc.

In recent organizational development programs, there has been conspicuous emphasis on the quality of personal and professional autonomy. Witness the "autonomous work group." To be sure, every responsible manager wants employees to develop wholesome and functional autonomy. However, there is the very real concern that increased autonomy benefit the organization. The decision of an employee to advantage the company depends on the conspicuous and mutual relevance and consequences of the commitment. If there are few rewards for achieving and exercising new competencies, employees feel free—and even encouraged—to exploit the new competence more to their own advantage than the organization's.

Let me share a personal experience. In a visit to the Volvo Company in Sweden, I was privileged to meet with some managers and employees. On that lovely mid-June day, these people displayed an obvious nonchalance in response to questions regarding the use of extended vacations to accommodate excessive inventory. They seemed to be personally at ease with the decision because the costs of their "vacations" were borne by the Government-supported social system. There was no expression of personal or organizational ownership. Did the social system prevent employees from accepting the responsibility for being competitive? Was employee accountability limited to the quality of the product regardless of the costs? Were the eight-person autonomous work groups disadvantaged by the failure of a leader to share with them information about increasingly threatening global competition? The consequences of illiteracy about such realities are personally, professionally, and organizationally devastating, disenfranchising employees from knowing and owning the compelling reasons to change and denying them the opportunity to become accountable and organizationally competent.

Was Volvo management behaving responsibly when it did not educate employees about the fact that Volvo's manufacturing costs exceeded those of every other global manufacturer of automobiles? Did Volvo employees have the chance to learn that they take twice as long to make a car as Japanese workers and that Volvo's primary overseas market had shrunk by fifty percent? Had Volvo management convinced employees that their absence at no personal expense or jeopardy severely reduced the cost effectiveness of the individuals and the teams at Volvo? Was there any model for management teaching and employee learning? Was change their hope?

There is genuine merit in the concept of autonomy in the development of personal and organizational maturity. Without an autonomous decision to become increasingly competent, learning may be handicapped by too much support, protection, or sympathy. Personal autonomy is significantly increased by a continual check against realities. Both individuals and organizations are critically dependent on the audited rationality of their behavior. These experiences point out the importance of personal and organizational commitments that recognize, establish, and exploit competence in fulfilling mutual, competitive demands. Autonomously achieved competencies and accomplishments of employees and employee teams should be noted and celebrated in the organization's monthly accountability process.

In the Motorola world of over 100,000 employees, management is committed to educate all employees, insuring them the opportunity to recognize and develop the competence required by customers. When the company commits itself to education, the employees must commit themselves to increasing learning and competence. The process is best when employee's autonomous decisions to acquire new competence is matched by the company's commitment to define and support the enabling programs.

Competitive reality establishes that increased competence is not an option. It is a condition of employment. It is critical that employees recognize the opportunity and take the responsibility to become corporately literate and competitively competent. Motorola employees discovered that the two sigma level of quality was not sufficient and had to achieve new levels of competence to meet the customer required level of six sigma.

The prevalence of personal and professional commitment among all employees to change and become increasingly competent engenders an ambiance of advancing, experimenting, and discovering. Curiosity becomes the norm. The shortened lives of products, the shortened response time of new product development and turnaround, and increased expectations from customers create a contagious tempo, which may be a little frenetic at times, among employees, who become ever more poised and confident. Personal and organizational commitment to increasing competence directs industrial and community resources toward life-long education.

People often ask me how to sustain this commitment. For some people, an obvious answer is to turn to the unions to establish and assure contractually the continuity of mutual commitments. But unions, human organizations with their own agendas, are not necessarily the only answer. Neither does winning an award assure continuity, as organizations that have passed the rigorous tests for winning the Baldrige Award have discovered. Changing realities shifted the benchmarks without affecting organizational and personal competence. Eric Hoffer put it well: "In times of change, the learners inherit the earth, while the learned find themselves beautifully equipped for a world that no longer exists."

What is the relevance of Japan's dedicated practice of focusing attention on the *processes* of operations and relationships rather than accentuating the faults of individuals? The Japanese determination to save face addresses the predictable resistance to change and to personal commitment. In the work situation, their disciplined attention to continuous study, examination, and correction of the *processes* that inhibit performance energizes and renews their culture and economic power. What would be the implications for organizations if we continually studied, examined, and reinforced the *processes* of education, responsible ownership, accountability, and commitment to enable employees to perform at world-class levels? The possibilities would be endless. And I think you know now why I call Frost-Scanlon a *process*.

Commitment to the Principles and Processes

In many organizations, the leaders are not as firmly committed to the principles and processes of Frost-Scanlon, nor are they as integrated throughout the company, as at Motorola and the Donnelly Corporation.

In all organizations, changes of leadership are as predictable as changes in competitive demands of customers. Inasmuch as hierarchical structures place conspicuous dependence on the personal values and professional servant-leadership skills of the leader, the continuance of any established principles and processes is at risk when a new chief executive officer appears. If, then, there is genuine belief in, and support for, the concept of *literate opportunity ownership*, shouldn't there be an established process whereby employees can own the participative process in their company? Wouldn't such employee ownership reinforce the faithful implementation and the continuity of the programmed processes? Might it encourage even greater employee accountability and commitment in serving customers and capital investors as well as themselves? Is there a genuine relationship between organization survival and the survival of the participative process?

This issue is addressed at Herman Miller, Inc. by the use of the term, "employee owners," an identity reinforced by the financial relationship of profit sharing and their employee stock-purchase program. As a part of the participative program, the company audits customers' satisfaction and capital investors' returns as factors in the calculation of employee bonuses. The company often audits the opportunities for employees to participate and become owners in all senses of the word. The success of the Frost-Scanlon process depends on management's fidelity to the idea of servant leadership, which can enable employees to cope with changing competitive pressures as they work to satisfy the expectations of all investors—including themselves.

The following citation of the Corporate Conscience Award to the Donnelly Corporation illustrates the principle that once mutual commitment is established, there must be a process of alertness and responsiveness to the fidelity of the commitment. This award confirms the current genuineness of Donnelly's commitment to an employee participation process.

DONNELLY
Donnelly receives Corporate Conscience Award

April 23, 1992

Donnelly Corporation has won the American Corporate Conscience Award for Employer Responsiveness for 1992. Donnelly president Paul Kalkman accepted the award on April 9 at the Waldorf Astoria Hotel in New York.

114

. . . its innovative workplace policies which has been recognized by, among others, the authors of *The 100 Best Companies to Work for in America* and *Justice on the Job: Resolving Grievances in the Nonunion Workplace.*

In 1952, Donnelly instituted a version of the Scanlon Plan, which attempts to increase productivity by involving workers in the company.

At Donnelly, the profit-sharing plan covers all employees, and work teams (which elect their own leaders) set their production goals to meet the company-wide objectives. Donnelly incorporates these lower-level teams into a larger system of involving employees that it calls the Equity Structure.

Throughout the company, employees serve on committees that have real decision making authority, as opposed to merely an advisory role.

Participation, workteams were noted

At the awards ceremony, Donnelly was described in the Employer Responsiveness category as follows:

Donnelly Corporation, the leading supplier of mirrors and glass to the automotive industry, is committed to involving workers in its decision-making structure. Its profit-sharing plan covers all employees, and work teams (which elect their own leaders) set production goals to meet company-wide objectives. These teams are represented on the Donnelly Committee, which considers higher-level issues. This system ensures that employees have a voice.

I believe that this Corporate Conscience Award more effectively assures the effective continuity of Donnelly's participative process than the company's recent recognition in the top ten of *The 100 Best Companies to Work for in America*, the well-known ranking by Robert Levering and Milton Moscowitz. This award documents an established and active and *ongoing process* whereby management actively listens and responds to genuine contributions and commitments from employees, and both management and employees nurture a mutuality of ownership and accountability in satisfying customers.

CHAPTER SIX

THE CRITICAL FACTOR: INTEGRITY

In addressing the personal, professional, and organizational development of executive leaders, as well as managers, supervisors, and every employee, one factor is pervasive and unquestionably critical. It is a factor about which there is no confusion. It is either present, or it is absent. It is the keystone of personal, professional, and organizational fidelity in any situation, performance, practice, or relationship. The factor is integrity.

In considering any organization, integrity is the factor that a consultant searches for. It is a quality universally relevant. It is universally recognized, appreciated, respected, and hoped for. It is a quality with which primitive as well as sophisticated cultures are acquainted. It is a quality useful, even powerful, in human relationships in private and public situations. Its absence is quickly and easily sensed, though the consequences of its absence are not always immediate or predictable. The absence of integrity inhibits initiatives to explore or to establish constructive or extended networks of relationships. Personal survival becomes a priority in these situations, which encourages the practice of situational ethics.

Throughout this book, I have presented reality as a critically determinative factor. The binding circumstances of organizations and employees are their mutual, critical reality. I have emphasized the importance—the essential nature—of knowing, understanding, comprehending, and deciding to accept or reject that reality as a personal and organizational given. If the presence of integrity is obvious in the situation, an employee can proceed with freedom, conviction, competence, and commitment to perform, practice, and relate. If integrity is absent or doubted, an employee will wisely proceed with caution and will be alert to compromise, seduction, or rejection. The situation is an essential code-terminant of behavior. The degree and quality of employee participation, accountability, competence, and commitment are determined to a large extent by the presence of, absence of, or uncertainty about integrity.

Why is integrity so critical in leadership and in every employee's personal, professional, and organizational development? Integrity is the essential quality that determines, defines, articulates, and implements justice. Justice is the ultimate, but also the minimum, expectation in a civilized society. In *The Good Society*, Robert Bellak and his teams call justice "the first virtue of our social institutions." In recent tributes to the late Thurgood Marshall, his fight for justice outshone all of his other accomplishments. He singularly and doggedly guided Congress to extend to all citizens justice in education, jobs, and voting. At Marshall's funeral, Judge Ralph Winter called Marshall "the irresistible force for justice, the immovable object against injustice, and a warm, kind human being" (Gilliom, James O., *Contact* 10 February 1993, 4). Too often leaders claim the qualities of warmth and kindness without first becoming *advocates* and *defenders* of justice. As advocate and defender, Thurgood Marshall undertook to educate the Congress about the realities of present injustice, so that they could clearly see a need to change. In organizations, leaders must educate people about present injustice and inequity, so that everyone clearly understands the compelling need to change. This act demonstrates the leader's integrity.

On this subject, let me cite the poem "Liberty and License (Galatians 5:13)" by Walter R. Wietzke, a special friend and insightful theologian. Though it's long, it's well worth quoting in full.

Two extremes obtain, says the Lord, two extremes.
    One is corporateness without individuality,
    the other is individuality without corporateness.
Neither, by itself, says the Lord, is truth.

I do not want authorities to establish demeaning institutions,
    churchly,
    governmental, or
    academic,
    where true self-hood is lost.

But neither do I create individuals to live apart from society, and the
    responsible mantle citizens must wear.
There have been occasions where my single ones have been lost in the mass,
    in the herd, in the institution. I know them all, I remember them all;
        the empire in which my son was slain, the system that could
        not abide his word or mine,
      the church that would not receive the monk's assertion of faith,
        but had to be upheld by a tottering system of reward,
      the establishment east of Berlin where all profess to be brothers
        but disavow a common father,
      the establishment west of New York where all plead a common
        father but disavow their brothers.
I know them all. I remember them all. And I hate systems that destroy
persons.

But that is not the only sickness of this hour. A plague has returned that
once afflicted Galatia. It is "making license of liberty."

My spokesmen have described the liberty that is,
    "the Christian man is the perfectly free Lord of all, subject to none,
    but at the same time, the perfectly bound servant of all,
        subect to all."
    It is in that tension you are called to live!

But you have defamed it.
    You would solve the mystery of paradox—but will not,
    You would resolve the tension—but you should not,
    You would dissolve its authority—but you cannot,
For I have ordained it!

I walked among you in the form of a servant, yet you want to
    parade before me as masters.
    You hear the word "we are lords of all, subject to none,"
    you fear the word "we are servants of all, subject to all,"
    and, my yoke of discipleship that binds them goes unworn.

So what is mine to see?
>Regents' resignation!
>Campus consternation!
>Placard profanation, four-letter obscenities—
>in the name of "freedom!"

Tell me how you will create the great society by following the
>least of men.
Tell me how you will foster liberty by perverting it to license.
Tell me how you will save individuality by destroying society.

It is as I have told you. "When the unclean spirit is gone out of a man, a
>better spirit must move in. . . . If it doesn't, seven lesser spirits will,
>and the last state of that man is worse than the first."

Anonymity is the unclean spirit? So be it! But do you take unto
>yourself that spirit which brings identity? Seven others wait.
>Seven, I say. Count them:
>>Vanity,
>>Profanity,
>>Enmity,
>>Despising of authority,
>>Contempt for morality,
>>Idolatry,
>>Insanity.
>>Seven. Count them, Seven!

I have not called you to license, for in that error society and selfhood is lost.
I have called you to liberty, for in its truthful tension, society and
selfhood is found.

The consequences of a leader's failure to establish and manage these
"truthful tensions" are as predictable and devastating as Wietzke suggests.
Count them. Integrity is the quality required if we are to avoid corporateness. It is also the linchpin of the Frost-Scanlon process.

If we believe that no person is an island and "corporateness" is an
amalgam of "individuality" existing in the truthful tension of competitive
realities, leaders must identify the relationships critical and fundamental
to accomplishing economic, social, or political objectives. To do less is to

betray one's commitment to *advocate* and *defend* justice. Even though a relationship may be only dimly perceived—as employees remote from their customers and investors; laboratory professionals remote from their patients; or graduate students remote from their parents and research-granting agencies—doing justice to the expectations of these essential constituents (all in their own "truthful tensions") demands a continuous, conspicuous presence, exercise, and demonstration of integrity.

Let me give a personal experience from my consulting practice. In examining the quality of integrity with company executives, I have purposely explored the definitions, awareness, and applications of that necessary quality. In pursuing the subject initially as a personal quality, the executive's responses were easily and broadly discussed with personal references to themselves and their families. They expressed obvious enjoyment, fulfillment, pride, and commitment in the exercise of personal integrity. They reported integrity as a positive force with significant consequences, and they expected increasing personal value and family enhancements. These exchanges are not only heartwarming, but they seem to evince motivating forces that integrate their values and behaviors into accelerated efforts and commitments.

Enjoyable and reinforcing as these discussions of personal integrity are, the mention of professional integrity as these executives experience it in organizational responsibilities seems to shift our conversation to another mode. It has been surprising, even shocking, that the shift from personal integrity to professional integrity causes a conspicuous change of demeanor. From a positive, fluid, sometimes buoyant conversation, the body language and tone of voice become restricted, sober, and hesitant. The executive becomes more reflective, as if struggling to introduce or adapt the quality of integrity into professional life. It does not seem to be an easy transition. The most common qualification in making this transition is, "Oh, but that gets to be political."

Inasmuch as all of our relationships with people might be termed political, what is the element or what are the factors that cause or influence these markedly different responses? Is this the way it has to be? Are there serious consequences of this seeming basic disparity as the person actualizes integrity first personally and then professionally? In light of these questions, we might examine the positive and negative implications for the organization and its employees.

As stated earlier, I believe that integrity, like humility, is a quality that you either possess or you do not. If you have to ask about it, you have already lost it. Colleagues and subordinates are aware of and responsive to their leader's personal qualities, as well as the organizational milieu. In fact, colleagues and subordinates are insightful and appreciative of their leader's behavior and responses to the political realities of a given situation. They are keenly aware of the presence or absence of integrity. Anyone would hope that in a civilized society, integrity would be an accepted and expected standard for behavior. What can we do to assure that integrity is a personal and professional value established and exercised throughout organizations?

Begin with the president. Does the corporate mandate dictate that integrity shall prevail in the management of *all* four factors—the marketplace, physical resources, financial resources, and human resources? Do the external imperatives of customers in demanding the right job according to the competitive criteria of doing that job right substantiate integrity of performance quality and service? Do the imperatives of financial investors in demanding assured returns on their capital investments in facilities, equipment, and technology substantiate integrity in all of the operating practices and usage of materials and disposables? Do the imperatives of employees requiring a fair return on their improving literacy, ownership, accountability, and commitment substantiate and verify integrity in their relationships to the organization? Or are those relationships fraught with double-talk and political innuendo? Does the competitive edge justify unethical behavior?

If there is a genuinely determined, defined, and articulated requirement for management integrity, then the process of education must establish what that means in principle and practice. Then management must give every employee the opportunity to endorse integrity as a given, and every employee must take the responsibility for always acting with integrity. The clincher is that every member—personally, professionally, and organizationally—beginning conspicuously with the president, must be held accountable for the uncompromising exercise of integrity in performance, practice, and relationships.

The experience of the employees at the Ford Motor Company's transmission plant in Sharonville, Ohio, illustrates a process of accountability for integrity in performance. The leadership was shared by Tom McCaffree, General Manager, and David Miller, President of the U.A.W. Local. With complete candor and hard-earned credibility, Tom McCaffree confessed to the employees that he had been assigned the task of closing down the old facility within a period of seven years. In a tedious, volatile, and grudging process, management provided the employees the opportunity, and the employees officially took the responsibility through the union, to satisfy customers with superior quality performance and services and to satisfy Ford corporate officers with superior returns on their investment, even when compared to more recently built and equipped facilities. It was not an easy situation in which to introduce and convincingly demonstrate personal and professional integrity because of the long-standing adversarial relationships and corporate politics. The integrity of the leaders was a most significant factor in salvaging the operation and assuring its continuing success. Among the many innovative ways of establishing and maintaining integrity throughout the company was a letter signed by McCaffree and Miller and posted in every department stating that every employee had the opportunity and the responsibility of stopping the production line with the supervisor any time that the quality deviated from specifications. On one occasion, when employees felt that management was hedging on the quality demands, union leaders staged a sit-down in the lobby outside Mr. McCaffree's office. The employees had accepted ownership of mandated quality as well as the participative process of influencing a decision in their area of competence. The official mutual commitment established the opportunity and responsibility to fulfill the situational ethics of personal, professional, and organizational integrity. The result of this total commitment has been the survival and success of this older facility in preference to newer and more technically sophisticated facilities at Ford.

After working many years with special clients who in time became more interested in the challenging questions around personal and professional integrity and servant leadership rather than the prescribed answers of a consultant, I sincerely believe there is genuine interest in recognizing, establishing, and fulfilling the unknown and untapped potential of integrity. I also recognize more clearly than ever the powerful and insidious interference of political forces and intrigue that inhibit the exercise of integrity and thwart the achievement of justice.

I have been encouraged, however, by the sincere study and reflection of selected executives who have accepted the challenge of becoming more conspicuously perceived as not only more qualified executives, but also more exemplary models of personal and professional integrity and values. I believe the unexpected popularity of Max DePree's two bestsellers, *Leadership Is An Art* and *Leadership Jazz*, supports this observation. It is true, many executives seem to enjoy privately discussing their values more than courageously implementing them. I sincerely believe the Frost-Scanlon processes not only incorporate personal and professional integrity and the other principles, but also genuinely require an organizational commitment to implement them.

Organizational Integrity: An Answer

I would like to suggest an answer to the dilemma in which employees experience the stressful contradictions between their personal commitment to integrity (individuality without corporateness) and the organization's sometimes inconsistent practice of integrity (corporateness without individuality) with customers, investors, and employees themselves. The answer is built into the principles and processes of the Frost-Scanlon process. The proof and exercise of organizational integrity is the conspicuous personal and professional public accountability modeled, led, and executed by the chief executive officer. The leader has the singular and conspicuous responsibility to chair and aggressively lead this exercise of public accountability. The process is the leader's unique and essential built-in instrument. The chief financial officer or the vice president of human resources is not an acceptable surrogate. The chief executive officer must assure, demonstrate, and document conspicuous, equitable accountability throughout the company in *what* people do, *how* they practice their competencies, and how they facilitate and capitalize on mutual relationships. Employees are quick to detect a lack of equitable accountability. They are especially insightful as to the presence or absence of personal and professional integrity. Organizational leaders must showcase integrity as the heart and essence of accountability by everyone, everywhere, all the time.

Consequently, the criteria for accountability must be obviously valid and reliable, believable and relevant. Such criteria must be based on reality—the reality experienced by customers, capital investors, and employees. The establishment of such a database is the essential and uncompromising instrument of the chief executive officer in aggressively executing the organization's regular public accountability process.

A regularly scheduled accountability meeting opens the leader to all investors' questions challenging organizational integrity in performances, practices, and relationships. (For example, production employees might challenge the sales department about deep discounting. Salespeople might challenge the development engineers to come up with a solution for the customer's problem—not just another product. The financial people might question the rationale for operating expensive equipment on only two shifts. Employees throughout the company might challenge the timeliness, helpfulness, and accuracy of the data provided.) The chief executive officer should conspicuously identify and challenge the executives of finance, development, operations, human resources, and sales and marketing for specific accountability in their areas of responsibility. The leader must make it clear that their responses are required not just to placate himself, but to address pointedly the issue or question of the challenger. It is the questioner who must be satisfied with the response, not the chief executive officer. In fact, the leader is in an advantageous position to evaluate the executives' answers for himself, the challenger, and the organization. The challenge may raise implications that are broadly relevant to the organization.

This process and discussion focus on what happened last period: why did it happen? Was it off target? on target? ahead of schedule? What are the consequences? What are management and the organization now committed to do? Improvements of performances, practices, and relationships are always on the agenda. In large companies, where employees may be scattered in a number of locations, a videotape of this "accountability occasion" can communicate the importance of the meeting to the entire company. The meeting should create a real picture of the chief executive officer holding the entire organization accountable for achieving its mandate. Now again, the leader must keep in mind the definition of a leader: the person perceived as the best means available to get the followers where they need to go at a particular time. Leader is a proactive role. Meeting this definition is genuine evidence that the chief executive officer is becoming more competent. The leader must provide personal, professional, and organizational perspectives that only he can provide. This unique contribution in the process of accountability is essential, whether the leader heads an industrial company, a college or university, a restaurant, or a congregation. There is a larger, changing world of vision and challenging expectations to which the leader is privileged by his office. The employees not only need that perspective, they deserve it, as evidence that their leader is growing not only *on* the job, but also *in* the job.

The operating data are not vague. The information must be reliable and current. Customers' demands for superior quality products and services should be continuously audited by their *registered* satisfaction. The database of the financial investment for publicly owned companies is available every day in the *Wall Street Journal.* The database describing employees' literacy, skills, and commitment is a matter of company record, with reports on such personal items as attendance, lost-time accidents and safety records, fringe benefit costs, on-time shipments, errors in shipments, productivity of departments, optimal capacity and efficient use of equipment, and turnaround times for new products. These specific data of accountability enable the leader to know and address the performance records as they relate to the demands of customers. The accountability process must be a visible and continuing documentation of integrity and justice for all members of the organization.

Another experience illustrating the professional consideration of the process of accountability is provided during consultations with hospitals. These clients quickly dismiss the preceding proposition of integrity's link to accountability as inappropriate and irrelevant. They claim that their institutions—hospitals, clinics, franchised service chains, or universities—are too different and too complex for such a process. They claim they are unique because they are committed to research, or teaching, or public service. Yet is there any industrial company that does not carry out research in developing new and better solutions for products and practices? That does not teach customers or clients about its products and services and employees, in continuous job training? And serves the public by getting to the marketplace sooner with superior performance and better products? I would argue that the three mandates of service institutions—research, teaching, and service—pertain equally to industrial companies. The need for literacy, participation, equity, and competence is as urgent in service institutions as it is in industrial organizations.

If research is a major function and commitment of an organization, aren't there criteria for performance, practice, and relationships that ought to be met? What are the realities of a research situation that are the primary province and raison d'être for that institution? Are there granting agencies that have a real interest in the researchers doing the right job? (Is the right job to research causes, cures, and treatments for AIDS or cancer rather than for diabetes or Alzheimer's disease? Is the right job energy conservation, atom splitting, or waste management?) And what are the criteria for doing the research job right? If research is a genuinely mandated function of the institution, then the institution has good reason to identify and integrate its researchers in their corporate responsibility, accountability, and commitment. Too often research and development are protected under different performance criteria, an

126

arrangement that may seriously handicap researchers, even disenfranchise them from the expertise, support, and collaboration of other members of the organization.

Equally important, this professional isolation prevents the organization's leader from fulfilling his responsibility to enable the researchers to demonstrate and authenticate their personal and professional integrity in achieving their institution's objectives and mandate. The recent scandals involving administrative manipulation of research moneys at prestigious universities are just one illustration of how devious management of research can become. Certainly personal and professional administrative integrity were grossly absent.

The teaching profession has been respected for accepting the responsibility of developing the literacy and competencies of our children as they prepare for changing global realities. In hindsight, I believe as parents we have delegated or even abandoned our opportunities and responsibility to enable our children to achieve their intellectual and professional skill literacies for survival and success. Consequently, the criteria for academic performance, practices, and relationships are vague and seldom vigorously shared and owned by the parents or community at large. Historically, as citizens, we have paid our dues by voting to sustain or increase funding for education. It may be that the general and recent resistance to approving annual millage requests is a predictable consequence of the absence of accountability for the equities of students, professionals in teaching and administration, parents, and the general public. The criteria for evaluating academic programs are further clouded by postponing judgment until students begin to apply their learning to their lives and careers.

We are awakened by the report that twenty-eight million employable Americans are unable to read a "help wanted" sign. Our current national literacy level is tenth among the industrial nations. In this predicament, the consequences are certain: People are not responsible, not accountable, not competent, and not committed. Our industrial and service institutions, as well as our society at large, are paying the price for the failure of educational institutions to establish the right job and the criteria for doing that job right. Because educational institutions, as well as service and industrial organizations, do belong to us as citizens, it is even more important that we citizen-owners become literate as to the global culturally competitive realities and thus own the problem. In this framework, I would recommend that we attack the process and not the people in evaluating and correcting the faulty system.

127

The third mandated commitment of service organizations (after research and teaching) such as universities and research-teaching hospitals, is the delivery of services. The extension services of the land-grant universities into agriculture are well known. Certain hospitals, like the Mayo Clinic and Johns Hopkins Medical Center, are nationally recognized for their unique medical services. Inasmuch as these service institutions have clients, patients, or extensive agri-businesses, a rational database from the end-users is key to evaluating the services received. The principle of equity and the process of accountability are appropriate and essential for all of these institutions. Only the integrity of the leadership and of the sophisticated professionals, together with valid and reliable data from end users, can move these institutions toward improved performances, practices, and relationships.

The point that I would like to suggest is that even in nationally prestigious service institutions, the four principles of management and the processes outlined in the Frost-Scanlon process are appropriate. The current public exposure of educational and medical institutions to penetrating financial examination and to critical challenge of the access to and availability of service suggests that innovative ideas and proven experiences may be worthwhile to study and explore. How long can these institutions ignore the changing realities of our economy, society, or political world? Where is the leadership—within or without the institution—that determines, defines, and articulates *today's* right job and the *global* criteria for doing the job right? Who is the leader among these sophisticated professionals who can convince them that their personal and professional past performances, practices, and relationships are inappropriate, inadequate, and may be truly obsolete? Can anyone convince them that change is their and our only hope? The sequel to these questions is the challenge: Do we have the will to earn an opportunity and a rightful place in this changed and changing world? Have we squandered our inheritance? Can we retrieve our national legacy of institutions of the people, for the people, and by the people? Can we recover the legacy of a free-enterprise system that recognizes the dignity of each person and challenges the potential of every person? The legacy of a unique nation that welcomes heterogeneity and enables the differences to become included and fruitful? The legacy of a nation where right is more important than might?

I sincerely believe that integrity is the answer to these questions. It begins with the *personal* commitment to exercise integrity in all performances, practices, and relationships. It advances to the expected greater *professional* commitment to exercise integrity in all performances, practices, and relationships. It culminates in the essential, mutual *organizational* commitment (of families, companies, institutions, and society) to exercise integrity in all performances, practices, and relationships.

Leaders have a special role to play in showing faithfulness to a commitment to integrity. Steadfast accountability is the fulfillment of integrity. When leaders provide a believable vision that change is our only hope for doing the right job and the job right, they are faithful to families, schools, factories, offices, universities, hospitals, and even to nations. When leaders *advocate* and *defend* the concepts of justice and accountability, they are faithful to the integrity of organizations and the people who follow them.

Chapter Seven

Synopsis and Implementation Outline

A t the beginning of this book, I outlined four principles of the Frost-Scanlon method of participative management and the four processes that I have found to be effective and efficient in implementing these principles. My clients over the years have been colleagues in defining, developing, and authenticating the effectiveness of these ideas in a wide range of organizational applications. The original outline showed the priority and sequence among the four principles and their four processes.

Now that I have discussed the ideas behind the principles of identity, participation, equity, and competence and have shared a range of examples of how various organizations have put them into practice, I would like to present an outline that includes the specific content and procedures for implementing the Frost-Scanlon process of participative management. I trust you recognize and agree that my clients and I have come a long personal and professional distance in defining this eclectic personal and organizational development process. I am sharing our findings to this point in time with the confidence that change is our only hope and that education is still our most promising investment in achieving change.

As you work through the outline, notice the consistent theme of confronting change throughout the organization. As the Frost-Scanlon process is implemented, the principles of identity, participation, equity, and competence will build and integrate. Their effects will mount. The processes essentially will capitalize on the skills—first of literacy, then of ownership, then accountability, and finally commitment. The sequence of these principles is not accidental.

The persistence of the three steps of the ownership process—opportunity, responsibility, and influence—suggest their effects on employees' awareness, insight, involvement, and commitment. As the organization comes to grips with change, the continuous and conspicuous role of the leader in defining and articulating the principles and implementing the processes is not optional. My own experience and the experiences of many of my client organizations have proved to me that the Frost-Scanlon process does fulfill the requirement that every business, organization, and institution be rightly judged by its products and services and that it face scrutiny and judgment as to its humanity.

We have discussed together the historic settings and the Scanlon Plan programs of the 1950s and 1960s. We have examined the evolution of the principles of the Frost-Scanlon process, beginning with the primary element of identity. We have activated its definition as literacy about personal, professional, and organizational realities. We have documented

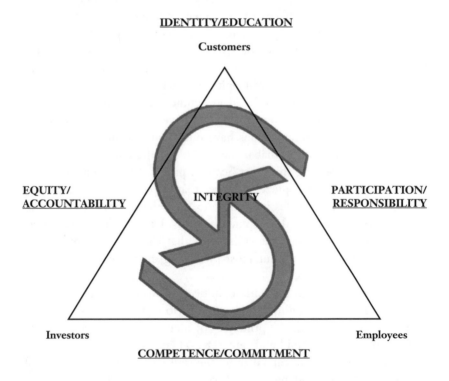

Figure 13. Frost Scanlon Process Diagram

132

literacy as it has become more urgent and compelling, not only for individuals, but also for organizations in their survival and their continuity of growth, maturity, and success.

I am convinced that education was and is the most promising process for gaining literacy, particularly when educators (both in academic settings and organizational ones) truly teach and students truly learn. Education can show that past performances, practices, and relationships are no longer appropriate or adequate. Education can identify present competitive realities as compelling reasons to change. Change has become the most promising action, if not the only hope, for future survival and success. We have reviewed the four necessary steps in a leader's effective teaching and the students' efficient learning: to know; to understand; to comprehend; and to accept the facts as personal and organizational givens. The role of a leader in education is paramount and is best functionally described by this definition: a leader must be perceived by the followers as the best means available for getting them where they need to go at a particular time. The organizational mandate is the most effective instrument for the leader to use in convincing all members of the organization that undeniable external imperatives are constantly imposed upon the organization. The efficacy of the mandate-education process can be proven only by the 90 percent-plus literacy score on the straw vote, the Quiz You Cannot Fail.

We have developed and implemented a specific definition of the second principle, participation: the opportunity that only management can provide, and the responsibility that only employees can accept, to influence decisions in their areas of competence. The four elements of participation are specific in sequence and purpose: management must provide the opportunity; employees must accept their responsibility; everyone must exercise influence in their respective areas of competence upon decisions that fulfill essential corporate objectives; and finally, participation must become an organizational reality and a way toward personal and organizational development. The process of implementing participation results in a real expression of a cherished American democratic principle—ownership—a kind of relationship that the free-enterprise system has advocated and made possible. Our principle of participation, if genuinely and fully implemented, will develop that process of *organizational ownership* by all employees for the common good, a competitive requirement for survival and success.

The third principle, equity, as I have described the concept, is not restricted to the usual financial meaning. Equity today should be based more on functional justice in performance, practices, relationships, and rewards. Its existence is always in jeopardy. It is a uniform expectation of all three participants in an organization or institution: the customer/patient/student, the capital investor, and the employee. The burden of assuring equity lies equally on management and employees.

The process of equity assurance depends heavily on the assumption of accountability among employees. The blatant demands of customers and capital investors require a structured, public, and regular process of accountability, an official clearinghouse that reconciles all accounts. This sophisticated data-based process of accounting does not simply certify the past. It reveals and comprehends the present and wisely anticipates the changing future. Conspicuous and regular accountability enables a leader to manage the four parts (customer/marketplace; physical resources; financial resources; and human resources) of any leader's assignment, to satisfy the external imperatives of competition, and to authenticate personal, professional, and organizational integrity to customers, shareholders, and employees, as well as to the industry and the community.

The fourth principle, competence, has too long been relegated to the lowest priority by individuals and organizations. Competence has not been managed by or for employees by either organizations or unions, as is documented by America's rate of skill illiteracy. Historically and until recently, organizations put no premium on lifelong personal or professional literacy or education. In fact, neither competency nor incompetency was well managed. More cruelly, competencies or improved competencies were often forgotten in expedient solutions to a company's immediate problems. Thus, there was no reason to commit oneself to becoming competent or more competent, even though competence is an early and a lifelong requirement for survival, fulfillment, and success. Without the opportunity or the personal and organizational commitment to change, employees working lifetimes have become personal tragedies and organizational and societal miscarriages of justice. Therefore, the commitment to become competent is the essential process for assuring personal self-worth. The organizational commitment to every person becoming competent, as illustrated by the Motorola Corporation, is a reasonable investment in establishing and maintaining global economic and political membership.

In conclusion, what have the Frost-Scanlon personal and organizational development principles become? They are not a plan, for though they have a goal, they do not have an end. They have fundamental importance in the effective and efficient sequential development of every employee, president, and chief executive officer. They can become a healthy part of the ongoing life of organizations and individuals. I believe these same principles and processes serve companies and institutions as organic units in their continuing commitment not only to survive but also to excel.

The principles and their processes substantiate the special tenets of our American heritage—education, ownership, justice, and commitment—in a free-enterprise system of the people, for the people, and by the people.

Change is our only hope—personally, professionally, and organizationally. It is not simply an experience of renewal. In all relationships, humanity depends on integrity conspicuously exercised, personally, professionally, and organizationally—in that order. Integrity is not selfish or self-serving, and therefore its exercise is conspicuous. The Frost-Scanlon process cannot assure integrity. It does provide the opportunity to advocate, defend, and implement the exercise of justice in every person's performance, practices, and relationships. Truly, the Frost-Scanlon process provides the basis from which leaders and followers can develop a rational working environment, can recognize the dignity of each person, and can challenge the integrity and competence of each person in fulfilling the competitive requirements of the organization's customers, investors, and employees.

Changing forever gives us the continuing opportunity to become responsible for making a difference.

Implementation Outline—Personal, Professional, and Organizational Development

IDENTITY

Corporate Approval to Explore Need to Change and Potentials of Innovative Participative Management

Organization's Mandate Development (The Company Story)
Doing the Right Job (Effectiveness)
Doing the Job Right (Efficiency)

Past Performances, Practices, and Relationships: Inadequate
Present Competitive Realities: Compelling Reasons to Change
Future Survival and Success: Must be Earned

IDENTITY AND PARTICIPATION

Opportunity (Executive Staff Development: The Company Story)
Knowing the Organization's Mandate
Understanding the External Competitive Imperatives
Comprehending the Personal, Professional, Organizational Consequences
Responsibility
Acceptance with Competence, Contributions, and Commitment
Influence
Confidential Straw Vote

Report to Corporate Officer
Executive Team's Acceptance of Organization's Mandate
Corporate Approval of Organization's Mandate and Authority to Proceed

Opportunity (Education of All Employees by Echelons—The Company Story)
Knowing the Organization's Mandate
Understanding the External Competitive Imperatives
Comprehending the Personal, Professional, Organizational Consequences
Responsibility
Acceptance with Competence, Contribution, and Commitment
Influence
Confidential Straw Vote
Are there compelling needs to change?
Are there genuine opportunities for improvement?
What is in it for you?
Are you willing to elect an Ad Hoc Committee to work with management to develop a company proposal for change?

Opportunity (Ad Hoc Committee Development of A Company Proposal)
Responsibility
Education Subcommittee
Participation/Ownership Subcommittee
Accountability Subcommittee

Report to Corporate Officer
Ad Hoc Committee Proposal with Chief Executive Officer and Committee Members
Acceptance of the Proposal and Official Endorsement by the Corporation

Opportunity (Education of All Employees by Echelons—The Ad Hoc Committee Proposal)
Knowing the Ad Hoc Committee's Proposal
Understanding the Processes of Education, Ownership, and Accountability
Comprehending the Personal, Professional, and Organizational Responsibilities
Responsibility
Acceptance of Ownership and Accountability of the Proposal Processes
Influence
Confidential Straw Vote

IDENTITY, PARTICIPATION, AND EQUITY

Opportunity: Establishment of the Accountability Process for Customers, Capital Investors/Owners, and Employees
Responsibility: Personal and Public Implementation of the Personal Professional, and Organizational Accountability

IDENTITY, PARTICIPATION, EQUITY, AND COMPETENCE

Opportunity: Determining the Right Job—Personal, Professional, Organizational
Defining the Competitive Criteria of Doing the Job Right— Personal, Professional, Organizational
Responsibility: Assuring and Enabling Competence in Doing the Right Job and Doing the Job Right—Personally, Professionally, and Organizationally
Influence: Personal, Professional, and Organizational Commitment to Continually Become Competitively Competent and Accountable in Performance, Practices, and Relationships

SUGGESTED ADDITIONAL READINGS

Anonymous. "An Informed Employee Is a Better Employee." *Employee Relations and Human Resources Bulletin*, 21 November 1991, Report No. 1748, 1-3 [Report on Trans-Matic Manufacturing Company].

Armstrong, D. *Managing By Storying Around: A New Method of Leadership*. New York: Doubleday, 1992.

Davenport, R. "Enterprise for Everyman." *Fortune* 41(1) (1950): 51-58.

Deinard, C. PREPARE/21 at Beth Israel Hospital (A). Harvard Business School, Case 9-491-045, Boston, Massachusetts, 1991, and Case 9-491-046, Boston, Massachusetts, 1991.

DePree, H. *Business as Unusual*. Zeeland, Mich.: Herman Miller, 1986.

DePree, M. *Leadership Is an Art*. New York: Doubleday, 1989.

———. *Leadership Jazz*. New York: Doubleday, 1992.

Donnelly, J. F. "Participative Management at Work." *Harvard Business Review* (January/February 1977): 117-27.

Driscoll, J. W. "Working Creatively with a Union." *Organizational Dynamic* (summer 1979): 61-80.

Fisher, K. K. "Management Roles in the Implementation of Participative Management Systems." *Human Resource Management* 25(3) (fall 1986): 459-79.

———. "Managing in the High Commitment Workplace." *Organizational Dynamics* (winter 1989): 1-15.

Frost, C. F. "The Scanlon Plan: Anyone for Free Enterprise?" *MSU Business Topics* (winter 1978): 25-33.

————. "The Scanlon Plan at Herman Miller: Managing an Organization by Innovation." In *The Innovative Organization: Productivity Programs in Action*. Edited by R. Zager and M. Rosow. New York: Pergamon Press, 1982.

————. "Participative Ownership: A Competitive Necessity." *New Management* 3(4) (1986): 44-49

Frost, C. F., J. H. Wakeley, and R. A. Ruh. *The Scanlon Plan for Organization Development: Identity, Participation, and Equity*. East Lansing: Michigan State University Press, 1974.

Gardener, J. W. *Self-renewal: The Individual and the Innovative Society*. New York, NY: Harper and Row, 1963-64.

Graham-Moore, B., and T. L. Ross. *Gainsharing: Plans for Improving Performance*. Washington, D.C.: Bureau of National Affairs, Inc., 1990.

Greenleaf, R. K. *Servant Leadership*. New York: Paulist Press, 1977.

Hall, J. *The Competence Connection*. Woodlands, Tex.: Woodstead Press, 1932.

————. *The Competence Process*. Woodlands, Tex.: Teleometrics International, 1980.

Lawler, E. E., III. *The Ultimate Advantage: Creating the High Involvement Organization*. San Francisco: Jossey-Bass, 1992.

Lesieur, F., ed. *The Scanlon Plan: A Frontier in Labor Management Cooperation*. Cambridge, Mass.: M.I.T. Press, 1958.

Levering, R., and M. Moskowitz. *The 100 Best Companies to Work for in America*. New York: Penguin Books, 1994.

Likert, R. L. *New Patterns in Management*. New York: McGraw-Hill, 1961.

McGregor, D. *The Human Side of Enterprise*. New York: McGraw-Hill, 1960.

Miller, C. S., and M. Schuster. "A Decade's Experience with the Scanlon Plan." *Journal of Occupational Behavior* 28 (1987): 167-74.

Moore, B. E., and T. L. Ross. *The Scanlon Way to Improved Productivity: A Practical Guide*. New York: John Wiley & Sons, 1978.

O'Dell, C. *People, Performance and Pay*. Houston, Tex.: American Productivity Center, 1987.

Rabkin, M. T., and L. Avakian. "Participatory Management at Boston's Beth Israel Hospital." *Academic Medicine* 267(5) (1992): 289-94.

Ramquist, J. "Labor-Management Cooperation—The Scanlon Plan at Work." *Sloan Management Review* 23(3) (1982): 49-55.

Scanlon, J. N. "Adamson and His Profit-sharing Plan." *American Management Association*, Production Series Number 172, 1947.

————. "Profit Sharing under Collective Bargaining: Three Case Studies." *Industrial and Labor Relations Review* 2 (1948): 58-75.

Scanlon Plan Associates. *The Scanlon Plan: A Better Way* [video]. Lansing, Mich.: Scanlon Plan Associates, 1987.

Schuster, M. "Gainsharing: Do It Right the First Time." *Sloan Management Review*, (winter 1987): 17-25.